A Winning Faith

The Margaret Court Story

Barbara Oldfield

Sovereign World

Sovereign World Ltd
PO Box 777
Tonbridge
Kent TN11 9XT
England

ISBN 1 85240 101 X

Scripture quotations are from the AV, Authorised Version of
the Bible, © Crown copyright, unless otherwise stated.

NKJ – New King James Version of the Bible, © copyright
1983 Thomas Nelson Inc., Nashville, USA.

Typeset by CRB (Drayton) Typesetting Services, Norwich
Printed in England by Clays Ltd, St Ives plc.

Contents

Foreword

If you flip through tennis record books, as I do many times in so many commentary boxes around the world, you eventually come upon a list headed: ALL TIME WOMEN'S GRAND SLAM LEADERS. (For the uninitiated, that means the players who have won the most numbers of the four big international championships – the Australian, French, Wimbledon and US, in calendar order.) Comfortably top of that list is the name of Margaret Court (Australia), followed by Martina Navratilova, Billie-Jean King, Doris Hart and Helen Wills-Moody.

When Margaret was all-conquering, it was before my broadcasting days, and I was writing about tennis for the London Daily Mail. So I got to know her, and her game, slightly more than at a surface level. One thing I particularly noted about her was that on Sundays, wherever she was, she went to Mass before she played her matches. I pondered on that fact because that was not the habit of most champions.

So I observed and reported on in the Daily Mail, the slings and arrows and golden triumphs that came upon this genuinely 'nice' girl with rather more interest than usual.

And so the years hurried on, and Margaret met and married big, affable Barry and I had new stories to tell about a whole new family. Then, one day, I read on the wires that Margaret Court, back home in Australia, had committed her life to Christ, and I wondered...

However some years later I heard that Margaret had become what the tabloids (and those who should know better) sloganise as 'a born-again Christian'. (I say 'sloganise' because it is my experience to this day that very few people outside the broad church-going fraternity – and often not many of them – know what this biblical phrase really means.)

My response to that news was joy, and coupled with it a concern for Barry. I, like Margaret, had grown to know that the word of God, believed with true faith, releases his power. I also knew for myself that some family and friends can appear to become alienated by this. Imagine, then, my sheer delight to find that Barry, too, had come to this place of faith, and that, when we all met up at the French championships in Paris a few years later, we were as one in faith in Jesus, though we might use different ways to express the same truths.

I am therefore delighted that this book has been written. I found it stimulating and challenging. Having witnessed Margaret praying for healing of the sick in my own church and seeing a powerful outpouring of the Holy Spirit I am convinced that her life, given in service to Christ, will touch the hearts and lives of many. I also believe that this book will be used to interest, encourage and challenge readers to find the same faith as Margaret – a 'winning faith'.

She so obviously has a 'peace beyond understanding' and I know that God will continue to use her, and reveal himself to her because the Bible says in Jeremiah 29 *'You will seek me and find me, when you seek me with all your heart.'*

Margaret has that heart for God, and it beats for him with a passion. I commend this book to you. When you have read it pass it on to a friend – especially any who don't know Christ.

Gerald Williams
The Millmead Centre
Guildford
January 1993

Championship Record

Australian Open Singles
1960–66; 1969–71; 1971; 1973

Australian Open Doubles
1961–63; 1965; 1969–71; 1973

Australian Open Mixed Doubles
1963–65; 1969

Wimbledon Championships Singles
1963; 1965; 1970

Wimbledon Championships Doubles
1964; 1969

Wimbledon Championships Mixed
1963; 1965–66; 1968; 1975

United States Open Singles
1962; 1968–70; 1973

United States Open Doubles
1963; 1968–69

United States Open Mixed Doubles
1961–65

French Championship Singles
1962; 1964; 1969; 1970; 1973

French Championship Doubles
1964–66; 1973

French Championship Mixed Doubles
1963–65; 1969

Italian Championship Singles
1962–64

Italian Championship Doubles
1963–64; 1968

Italian Mixed Doubles
1961; 1964; 1968

South African Open Singles
1968; 1970–71

South African Open Doubles
1966; 1971

South African Mixed Doubles
1966; 1970–71; 1974

German Open Singles
>   1964; 1965; 1966

German Doubles
>   1964; 1965; 1966

German Mixed
>   1965; 1966

Federation Cup
The International Teams Championship
>   1963–65; 1968–69; 1971

Margaret won every single match she played in her singles encounters – 20 out of 20.

Introduction

Sport provides tremendous entertainment for there
is something intrinsically exciting about watching
battles of immense proportions being fought out with
only one of the two combatants – either an individual
or a team, being declared the winner. I for one,
always enjoyed winning. It was just the rarity of the
wins that spoiled that particular enjoyment. But that
could not be said of Margaret Court, who also
enjoyed winning, for it was only her losses that were
a rarity!

Although I was headed for the top in squash, being
the 5th ranked player in the world in 1982 before I
was forced to retire through illness, I never quite
made it to the winner's circle as often as she did. But
there were very few players in the world in any sport
who collected as many winning trophies as she did!
Her incredible record of sixty four grand slam titles is
almost unbelievable, but the records faithfully docu-
ment each one of those amazing victories.

One of my biggest mistakes in the last year was to
invite the 'Queen of Wimbledon' to play a fun game

of squash with me as a battle of the 'oldies'. It became very apparent even in the hit up that she was not used to having her opponent on the same side of the court, for the arc of her swing could cut a path from Perth to Sydney. Secondly, the back wall was not really a consideration for her as she preferred to forget any ball that slipped past her amazing reach to the back of the court. Therefore her whole intent was to dominate the central court area and put into effect her cut-off volley.

The years had done nothing to diminish her tenacity and determination. We could have been playing for the championship of the world as she ran for even the 'impossible' shots – at least I believed them to be – and even tried to volley away my drop shot winners! I had always thought of myself as the most competitive person I knew, but watching Margaret made me think again. It was not hard to see why she had won so many titles. She didn't know the meaning of the word quit.

Any ball that came anywhere near her was punched back into play with an awesome power generated by her lethal swing. It was the balls she hit just over my head that worried me the most! I exercised far more that day than I had expected to, as I skilfully kept away from her swing to avoid having my head neatly removed. I hoped her faith was high that day for she may have had to use it to its extreme and raise me from the dead should one of those full-bodied swings connect!

I am happy to report a narrow win that day as I

emerged life and limb intact. That Margaret had also become the 2nd ranked player in Western Australia squash during her 1966 retirement did not surprise me one bit. I have yet to be invited to play her at tennis but she has seen me 'playing tennis' and is obviously saving me from the embarrassment of having to decline her invitation. My less than firm tennis grip means that the shots I intentionally hit back over the net as sharp, accurate pin-point drives, go off on a 45 degree tangent with alarming regularity. The players on any adjacent courts are not usually impressed as I hit my ball into their game more times than I do my own. My racquet skills are best left with the game of squash!

Besides our common interest in sport, Margaret and I share a great spiritual affinity. It was in the family room of her home in 1980 that I gave my life to Christ. It was a wonderful day as the sun's rays cascaded playfully into the room creating a special lighting effect. Like most people I had experienced emotional and physical traumas of some magnitude before I realised that I could not make it on my own. These had been the catalysts in pushing me to my knees where I was in a great position to pray!

Within two months the immediate traumas had passed, so I took my life back again into the world, the flesh and the devil. Jesus had been my crutch, but now I was well again I had no intentions of going religious, for it excited me about as much as being ravaged by a dead sheep. It was unfortunate for me that I didn't make Jesus my wheelchair, for I was once again on the path to ruin although I did not see it at the time!

The best description I can give of my life over the next ten years was life on a roller coaster; sometimes up and sometimes down – it all depended on the circumstances. Winning made me happy, losing did not. It applied to sport and my life in general.

But through all these turbulent years Margaret was always there for me. She never criticised me or condemned me in any way for my numerous failings. It was as though she knew I would have to run the race my way; the theme song to hell could well be 'I did it my way'. I was certainly not living in any heaven on this earth. It was more like hell!

Finally the realisation that I had run from God instead of to Him in my greatest need came about as I saw the love of God at work in Margaret. It was her unchangeable advice always straight from God's word, her unconditional love and acceptance, and her refusal to give up on me knowing that the day would come when I would come home to God as His long lost 'prodigal son'.

Today I have come full circle. I no longer live in the fear and uncertainty of the world; I live in the faith and certainty of God. Since I made such a mess of it my way, it was obvious that His way was the only way to go if I was to enjoy success in every dimension of my life.

I became a part of the Margaret Court Ministries Inc. in 1991 for I have the same heart desire that Margaret has to see all the lost, lonely and hurting people in the world come to know Christ, their only source of strength and comfort in these turbulent times.

Our battle is not being fought out in any sporting arenas but on the streets of Perth, as we fight against the forces of darkness that keep people's eyes blinded to their need of a Saviour. Victory in winning souls is always sweet. There is joy unspeakable in being a champion for God.

The story I tell in the following pages is one of victory and defeat, for while Margaret was a winner in tennis she was not necessarily a winner in life. Her story will encourage you when you find yourself depicted in any of her experiences of fear, guilt and worthlessness, all of which she finally overcame. If you apply the same principles, you too will be able to overcome any areas of defeat in your own life.

At the back of the book is a small prayer that you may want to pray on the completion of this book. If you are the only person that prays this prayer through a conviction gained from reading this book, then I feel I have told the story well.

Barbara Oldfield
September 1992

Chapter One

Margaret Court Smith is without doubt the most successful tennis player of all time, amassing sixty-four grand slam titles. She won eleven Australian Opens, five US Opens, five French Opens and three Wimbledon Opens in singles: twenty one doubles and a further nineteen mixed doubles. If that was not enough she also won twenty five Italian, German and South African Opens in both singles and doubles!

She was only a teenager of seventeen when she began on the senior circuit in 1960 and was still playing fourteen years later, taking three Grand Slam titles in 1973, a remarkable achievement considering she had taken two years out. She had an amazing ability to come back from retirement and childbirth to fulfil certain goals she had, when many others would simply have quit!

She never knew how to quit right from the time of her birth in 1942; a time of war and great fear in Australia, for it seemed inevitable that the Japanese would invade the northern shores. But in Albury New South Wales, Maude Smith's greatest concern was not the war but whether she would safely deliver her fourth child in life-threatening circumstances. The battle was won as both she and her new daughter, named Margaret, went proudly home after the 'miracle' birth.

Margaret grew up with her mother being very fearful. The thought of having nearly lost Margaret at birth made her all the more determined that nothing would harm or injure her youngest child in any way – not that she wasn't as protective with all her children, for her fear was so intense it bordered on paranoia of strange people and places.

Unfortunately for Mrs Smith, Margaret developed at an alarming rate. She crawled, walked and climbed at an age when other babies were content to lie and be entertained. Her toddling years were like a nightmare for her fearful mother, and her pre-school years no better. Mrs Smith often thought she had given birth to another son as Margaret lived life at such a pace that she out-played and out-ran every other child – male or female – in the district.

The country life style of Albury suited her long-legged athletic disposition. She much preferred to be outdoors running, jumping, kicking or hitting a ball than to be inside passively playing with dolls!

All through primary school she felt she was wasting precious time. It took a real effort for her to sit for long hours in the classroom. For her, the school-room paled into insignificance compared to the 'outdoor' schoolroom where she learnt so much from her broad and vast 'hands on' experiences.

She loved nothing better than to hear the old school bell toll the close of day. By the time she was in the fifth grade all she ever wanted to do was to go out and hit a tennis ball, hour upon hour against any convenient wall, with apparatus that resembled a tennis racquet.

She lived for the weekends when there was no school. Her favourite pastime was to go fishing with her Dad along the banks of the beautiful Murray River. Large cod would often grace their dinner table through their successful trips. The Murray was her 'Mississippi' and she its 'Huckleberry Finn'. This river was endless in its possibilities. She would hide in its tangled old logs and gnarled reeds along its banks, drop from old tyres hanging from the trees into its cool waters during the oppressive heat of a summer's day, and fish its precious contents right out onto a plate.

Margaret had no real girlfriends. She was the leader, by virtue of her greater height, over a small gang of boys on which she constantly practised her leadership qualities. She was their 'Boadicea'; girls never acted like she did – she was bold and daring and she was just one of the guys!

The Smith family were not wealthy but there was an abundance of activity in their family home. Her Dad was the foreman in the local ice cream factory and her popularity rose markedly on Saturdays when the free ice creams came home with him.

But her mother was a champion worrier. She worried incessantly about every conceivable thing possible and if, by mistake there was nothing to worry about, she worried that she wasn't worried about something, for something bad was obviously just around the corner waiting to happen.

She was never at peace with her family and always feared the worst in every situation. The family would take hours to persuade her just to go for a drive with them but when she did she insisted that they take her straight home because she had left the stove on. Despite assurances to the contrary, Mrs Smith could not relax until she went home to invariably find that she had not. Fear gripped her life and imaginations of every dimension played havoc in her mind, developing into severe phobias.

Lawrence, Margaret's father was quite the opposite. He had a zest for life and loved nothing more than taking his youngest daughter fishing. He really didn't worry about much at all! Margaret was caught somewhere in the middle, as she learnt how to worry just like her mother and yet learnt how to relax and have fun without any care just like her father.

The gang under her control often played tricks which would have given Mrs Smith good reason to worry, had she known about them.

A curve in the highway, just on the outskirts of town, was a breaking point for the road trains before they came into town. It was also lined with large bushes in which the gang could hide out and wait for a driver to slow his truck. Once they heard the lowering of the gears they would quickly climb aboard the tailgates of the now slow moving road train to catch a ride to the next turn in the road. Daringly foolhardy, they held on like riders on a rodeo horse ready to jump off just before they entered the turn.

Then laughing and with the adrenalin freely pumping, they trotted back to do it all again.

At times they would take with them a large brown paper parcel and to break the monotony of the afternoon waiting for 'free rides', they would tie the parcel with string and throw it into the middle of the road.

Like fishermen perched on rocks, they waited patiently in the bushes for a bite; the parcel being the bait. They hid themselves in the bushes waiting for a motorist to be 'hooked' by their parcel. As the fast moving motorist approached, they often went past the parcel only to back up to see what it was. Of course once they backed up, the parcel mysteriously disappeared into the safety of the bushes by a hefty tug on the attached string. Outright laughter had to be compressed into suppressed giggles to avoid detection by the bemused motorists, who stood scratching their heads in bewilderment!

On one occasion a humourless fellow had seen the parcel disappear into the bushes and went in after it. The gang fled in all directions; their fleet footedness assuring their escape from the cursing, lumbering figure. They met as usual by the local river and daringly dropped into the water from the overhanging tree branches and then lay like sprawled out crabs in the sun to dry out their clothes before going home for tea. By the time she was eight Margaret had taken to 'tennis', which was hitting a hairless ball with a plank of wood against the garage wall. She recognised quickly she would need some hitting companions to make it much more enjoyable and to fetch the odd ball or two. So half the gang were ordered to volunteer their time to start hitting some balls with her on the road outside her home. Right across the road from her house were the twenty four grass courts of the Albury tennis club, but as they were for members only, she could only dream about the day when she would be able to play on them.

However, not being a member was not about to stop this gang from playing on them, because once Margaret felt her standard of play had progressed satisfactorily she led them onto the back court of the grass courts through a hole in the hedge. This hole she had managed to find one day while previous reconnaissance of the court had shown that three quarters of it was totally hidden from the club house by a magnificently located cypress tree with only the back quarter exposed. Here they could play to their hearts content if the ball didn't go to the back of the court. So she decided on this their first time, that she being head and shoulders over the rest of them, should station herself at the net to stop the balls from going through to the back. This of course meant she had to try to volley anything that came her way. Without knowing it she had begun to practise the very stroke that would mark her future dominance of women's tennis.

But here on this very first day and on this big

occasion she was anything but dominant, as the two balls they had, repeatedly went over her head to the back of the court, despite her urgings to the three boys on the other side of the net to keep them down a bit!

Each took a turn in retrieving the balls by crawling on their stomachs to the back of the court, keeping their heads well down all the time, and hoping the local professional Mr Rutter was not at that time fixing his eye on this outer court. Unfortunately for them he had already spied these 'illegal immigrants' on his courts, and was on his way to clear them off his beloved grass; every blade of which he treated with the same respect Jewish women have for their sons.

One look at them; with not a sandshoe between them nor anything that resembled white clothing, left him open mouthed. Their racquets were more like lethal weapons or relics from a lost age with the mishappen look of having spent all day in the sun and overnight in the rain.

'Clear off you young rascals' he ordered in a gruff but somewhat indulgent way. And scamper they did – in record time, exiting through the same hole that had been their entrance, trailing their interesting array of racquets with them. They knew – and he did too – that there would be another day. This fear of detection just made it that little bit more exciting!

Mr Rutter had appeared to be tough, but they noticed that he never once plugged the hole in the hedge. The gang were often unofficially on his courts.

Not long afterwards he began Saturday morning clinics for the juniors in the district. If the interest of Margaret and her gang were anything to go by, he felt the kids must be keen and ready for some type of formal tennis instruction. Indeed they were – and none keener than Margaret who was always the first to turn up with her old secondhand racquet in one hand, and her two shillings in the other, and with loads of determination!

Margaret had already changed her game from hitting with her natural left hand to her right hand, for the boys in her gang had teased her incessantly that there were never any good 'southpaw' players. Needless to say her backhand was always far more formidable than her forehand for she was on her natural side.

Tennis began to consume her: she lived only for the time when she could get out there and hit the ball on the court or against the garage wall, or even from a ball hanging from a rope in a tree!

It was a passion her teacher didn't share, as she confronted Margaret daily with the fact that she needed to get on with her studies and forget this 'tennis madness' as she called it. Tensions erupted the day she hauled Margaret in front of the class and demanded an apology from her for something she had not done. Margaret refused to apologise; she had told the truth and refused to give in to what she knew wasn't right. As the teacher seemed intent on severing her ear, Margaret bolted for the door and ran home determining she would never go back. She hated school and now it was threatening her love of tennis – that she couldn't bear! Indeed she didn't go back, despite her mother's tears and the headmistress's threats.

Three days later she attended school in Wodonga, Victoria four miles away but across the border from Albury, New South Wales. She had made history; going to school in two states without changing houses! Here the headmistress was supportive and greatly encouraging to Margaret, seeing her tennis talent as a great gift from God.

By now she had excelled herself in the tennis clinics run by Mr Rutter. He could see the talent in the youngster and he constantly worked with her himself. Most evenings he would hit with her and coach her, installing in her a new self-confidence. He never took any money for his lessons, as he knew the family couldn't afford it, so he let Margaret do little jobs around the courts. She actually painted the court lines, served drinks and even mowed the lawns. She never ever forgot his early valuable contribution to her life for it was his perseverance, persistance and sheer doggedness that went into her. As she moved to play in the country district tournaments, he would upbraid her if she won in three sets instead of two. 'You'll never win Wimbledon with that attitude' he would always say.

He organised many games for Margaret with the men in the club, for she eventually became so strong that no woman in the district could give her a solid match. They all complained that she hit the ball far too hard for a girl, a complaint that many of her future competitors would make in the years ahead.

This practise with the men would be invaluable, as Margaret was forced to develop an extremely powerful and penetrating serve to allow her to advance swiftly into the net. From here she looked to curtail the rally, for sustaining it would not be to her advantage as she was not as physically strong as her male opponents. Thus was birthed her dynamic volley, as she consistently punched away the usual cross court defensive return for a winner. By playing the men, she learnt very early to play in an aggressive attacking manner every time she took the court. This was the new style of tennis she brought into the game.

Frank Sedgeman, the Australian Open Champion in 1949 and 1950, prompted Mr Rutter to send Margaret to Victoria to trial her out in the girls under 19 championships, so that he could see her in action. He and Keith Rogers, a professional tennis coach, felt that she showed excellent potential. Therefore it was decided that Margaret should move to the city to further her tennis career.

A job was organised for her by Frank Sedgeman, and Margaret took up a position as a junior clerk in his office. He arranged to have her train at his Melbourne gym under the watchful eye of his head physical culturist Stan Nicholes, and to have coaching with Keith Rogers.

Margaret was only fifteen when she left her home to go to Victoria. She took a suitcase, a racquet and a hand sewn tennis outfit to be worn in her very first tournament. Her mother was devastated to think of her daughter going off to play tennis. Her father encouraged her all the way. Their tears at the railway station were hard to contain as they said their good-byes.

Margaret's move to Melbourne was not as traumatic as it might have been, for she was able to move into the same boarding house as her elder sister June. June had earlier moved to the city for her work, and she provided Margaret with the all-important family support. Margaret is aware that without June's encouragement she may never have realised her greatest ambition of becoming the first Australian woman to win Wimbledon. Whenever she felt a little discouraged or homesick, she kept that vision before her all the time. She disciplined herself to keep the picture alive in her imagination at all times; it was all she ever really thought about to any great degree. It was such a burning desire that it consumed every difficulty in the way.

Right from her first appraisal in the gym with Stan Nicholes, Margaret recognised that to become the best, she would have to be the fittest, strongest woman ever to play. One look at her twiggy frame confirmed that this meant a lot of hard, intense, painful work to achieve the strong skeletal structure she would require to play her powerful serve and volley game.

Stan devised a specific tennis movement and physical weight training program involving circuits. Keith Rogers went to work with Margaret, doing the same athletic conditioning she did, of long runs to strengthen her aerobic threshhold and short sprints to quicken her reflexes and increase her anaerobic uptake. Margaret became such a good sprinter that she was tempted to concentrate on athletics as a career. Thankfully for tennis she made the right choice! Both Stan Nicholes and Keith Rogers were always ready to help Margaret. She never forgot their input into her tennis for there was no monetary rewards: they simply did it to help a talented young Australian achieve her destiny.

Day by day, week by week, she trained so hard that even the men in the gym found it hard to keep up with her. As the slim figure of a young girl began to change into the shape of an athlete, Margaret was worried that she would lose her feminity. But assured by Stan that she did not have enough test-osterone, the male hormone, to develop bulging muscles, she kept on with the weight programme.

Slowly she gained competitive experience and by her sixteenth year, had managed to take all before her in most competitions, except for one other outstanding junior – Jan Lehane.

Then in 1960, just two and a half years after the shy teenager began her earnest preparation to contest the Australian title for the first time, she actually won it! Not only did she win it, but she also managed to beat the current world champion at that time, Maria Bueno, in three sets. She was delighted, but she could see the face of a beaming Mr Rutter saying 'You should have beaten her in straight sets if you want to be the first Australian to win Wimbledon.'

She was famous overnight, but with that victory came the enormous pressure to play up to that standard and to prove it was not just a fluke; a one-off victory she could never repeat. Immediately afterwards, during the New Zealand tour she lost the final of the New Zealand Open. For the first time she was playing under the pressure of an expectation that she should be winning even if she was not. Previously that had never worried her.

It was decided straight afterwards, that she had in reality won the Australian 'before' her time. As Frank Sedgeman related 'I knew she was good but not that good'. He had always told her he believed she could be the first Australian woman to win Wimbledon, but not even he had expected her to excel at such a rapid pace.

So, after consultations with the 'powers that be' – the LTAA – she was not selected to go on the tour with the rest of the Australian team in 1960.

She was devastated by this. It was a blow to her pride and she was severely disappointed not to be going overseas and have a chance to win Wimbledon. She had proved herself: this was grossly unfair.

The LTAA felt she was immature and needed more time. Margaret did use the time well, for she was so determined never to be left out again that she trained and conditioned herself to a physical perfection that would ensure she would never be left out again.

Chapter Two

Winning the Australian Open for the second successive year in 1961, assured Margaret of a place in the Australian team to tour Europe, England and the United States. The vision of Wimbledon was so much closer and she was still only a teenager. However, nothing could have prepared her for the nightmare tour she would endure under the authority of the Lawn Tennis Association of Australia's team manageress, Mrs Hopman.

Even before she left Australia's shores for the first time, Margaret had been a little apprehensive about Mrs Hopman's statement that she would bring the team home to show a profit on the budget allowance. Tennis in Australia, as in the rest of the world, was still an amateur sport, and appearance money for top players was about the only way a team could profit from touring certain countries. Margaret was aware that of the five women players on tour, she was the only one to hold a Grand Slam title – so where was the profit going to come from?

Their first stop in Monte Carlo at a luxurious castle

with servants, was like a fairytale world to Margaret; she had never lived in such luxury before. It did not hinder her game in any way however, as she went on to win the Monte Carlo Open.

But in France, their second scheduled city of tour, the 'Cinderella to riches' bubble burst, with the team being accommodated in third class hotels in Nice, Aix-en-Provence and in Paris. A continental breakfast of croissants and coffee were all they were allowed to have, for it was part of the cheap package deal. Margaret, who was used to a huge breakfast of a grill and eggs, toast, juice and cereal, did not relish this type of breakfast.

Finally in Paris they revolted, and ordered steak and eggs for dinner one night, instead of the usual hotel special. A stiff reprimand followed, and the meal expenses were taken from the players' own pockets! Margaret couldn't believe the treatment the players were receiving. She felt Mrs Hopman was going too far by not providing the correct food suitable for active athletes.

In London it grew worse. More cheap accommodation followed, miles from the playing courts. There was no allowance for the players to attend doctors, physiotherapists or masseurs for muscle soreness. Practise after practise session was ordered. This was no pleasure trip she had come away on: it was all hard work and there was no leisure time.

Margaret was tired and grew sick. She became dreadfully homesick as she had no-one on the tour to relate to. Her best friend and doubles partner Mary

Rectano, had the misfortune to badly injure her foot and had been sent back to Australia. It was felt it would be too expensive to keep her on the tour. No wonder this tour was going to return such a profit!

Margaret's first Wimbledon was fast approaching but so were the tired and listless symptoms that she had first noticed in Paris. Her nervous debut was made, as the very first match, on the centre court. She managed to win that day and played well enough to go right through to the Quarter finals. But the English press were out in force to find the achilles heel of the Aussie no. 1, and the extreme attack of nerves had not escaped their notice!

Margaret took to her bed. She was so depressed and despondent. This tour had been such a horrid experience and now she was actually physically ill. She competed in the doubles with her age-old junior rival Jan Lehane, only to lose to the Americans. Again she took to her bed. This time a doctor was called and she was diagnosed as suffering with glandular fever.

She spent the night of the Wimbledon Ball – the night she had dreamed about – in the University College hospital. She cried to think of her beautiful black and white dress, specially purchased for the occasion, still unpacked in her suitcase. She also cried because she felt really alone; her family and friends were thousands of miles away. She had dropped six kilos in weight and was a shadow of her former self.

A lonely nineteenth birthday was spent in the hospital despite the staff making her a birthday cake and

Neale Fraser and Rod Laver stopping by to cheer her up. She had lots of time during this period to think, and she decided that she would never again tour with the Australian team whilst Mrs Hopman was the manageress.

She only played one more doubles tournament, and that was in Germany, under pressure to make the budget more profitable by money guaranteed for her appearance. She loved the United States and enjoyed the crowds because they were so friendly and enthusiastic. It was also the last part of the tour; this was the homeward run and she knew her days of being treated so badly as a player were about to come to an end. She reached the semi-finals of the US Open – a magnificent effort after all she had been through, and which put her up there as one of the world's top four players.

Great controversy surrounded Margaret as she returned to Australia. The press had already caught hold of the friction and strike action of the Australian team on tour and Margaret's declaration never to go away again under these conditions.

The headlines boomed 'Teenage Tennis Star Defies Tennis Brass'. The commotion died down but the full impact would not come until months later, when Margaret faced the LTAA on her own in a full inquiry, as the other players refused to lend their support. However she was determined to hold her ground, and refused to compromise her position one bit.

As expected, with her third consecutive win in the

Australian title she was named to tour in 1962. She accepted, believing Mrs Hopman would not be named as team manageress. However a month later she was appointed. Margaret felt cheated and deceived by the false assurance given to her. Now she had to make a decision which could affect her own personal tennis career for the sake of certain principles she believed in. If she refused to tour, her amateur status may be affected because she would then be considered a professional. It was her against the establishment, as she decided to go it alone once again.

A Melbourne businessman, Robert Mitchell would come to her aid offering to finance this 'rebel with a cause' on a private tour. However the LTAA were not about to let their number one player slip away without a public censure which expressed confidence in Mrs Hopman, and deplored the embarrassment this had caused her. Another official publicly stated that he wished Margaret all the ill-luck in the world, and hoped she would lose every tournament she played in.

Despite all this furore Margaret coped quite well for she had a maturity well beyond her years; perhaps leaving home at fifteen had developed that, for she was confident she had done the right thing. She and Mrs Bill Edwards, the wife of the Queensland Tennis Association President, left for their own private tour one day before the official team left in April 1962.

However the pettiness of the LTAA would show

further, as on her first attempt to catch a practice match with one of the Australian girls, she was told that there was a ban on anyone practising with her. She was ostracised and cut off from all of them. Margaret's determination grew with this rejection but it still hurt her. She cocooned herself into an isolated world – her racquet alone would show them.

And show them she did. With a valiant Alf Chave, the Australian men's manager, by her side to help and support her, she won the Italian Open against her old rival Maria Bueno from Brazil, being the first Australian to do so. Mr Chave received a 'please explain' letter as to why he had supported her in light of the ban on Margaret. His simple but poignant reply – 'Because we are both Australians' – received no answer. Not surprisingly he was never appointed manager again.

From here she went on to take the French Open from Lesley Turner the official team's number one player. The road to Wimbledon was wide open. She had won ten tournaments in a row and could she now win this much coveted crown? She, of course, was the number one seed for the event having already won the Australian and French titles.

The press were merciless in their approach to her. The headlines said it all 'CAN SMITH WIN WIMBLEDON?' the headline questioned. 'SMITH'S CENTRE COURT NERVES' – for her last nervous showing at Wimbledon had not gone unnoticed. Every headline she read reinforced her own fears of failure.

In 1961 the Wimbledon draw only seeded eight players. Margaret's worst fears came to pass when she saw her draw for the first time. She drew the number three ranked American, Billie Jean King in the very first round. Again the press pounced. Seeing the bombastic openness of the American they played on it, and she was more than happy to admit that Margaret had all the pressure and that she had nothing to lose and everything to gain. And indeed she was right.

Further doubts would creep into Margaret's heart as the press hounded her further with constant questions about whether she was nervous playing Billie. She was, but of course she couldn't say so; their hint of upset had already marked her mind. It got so bad Margaret felt physically ill in the stomach; the nerves were back and she knew that she would not play all that well in this tournament. True to her own fears Margaret would create history by being the first no. 1 seed to be ousted in the first round of Wimbledon. This was the darkest and deepest despondency she had ever felt; it was even worse than last year's horror tour.

The next morning, after a sleepless night spent replaying and reliving every stroke she played, the morning headlines boomed her failure to the world. 'SMITH LOSES – WILL SMITH EVER WIN WIMBLEDON?' She knew how disappointed her family and friends would be at home and that only made her feel worse.

She felt she had failed herself, her coach and even her country.

Her mother consoled her daughter as best she could over the phone. Although she was upset that she had lost, she was hoping that now Margaret would forget all this tennis madness and come on home. For the first time Margaret felt her mother may be right. In the last two years, although achieving some tremendous wins and being at many high points, the hurts, frustrations, rejections and disappointments were almost too much to bear. However it was only a temporary phase as telegrams, well wishes and flowers flooded her hotel room expressing disappointment in her loss but encouraging her that there would be another day. These people believed she still had what it took to be a champion. Champions always get back up from a blow; they don't stay down. And precious to her was the following letter she received from England's finest men's player, Fred Perry:

'Dear Margaret

The world seems a lonely place today. With hopes dashed so suddenly yesterday and the circumstances under which you were knocked out of the singles being so dramatic, I am sure you are a most unhappy person. Don't think for one moment you are as alone as you think, for there are many hundreds of thousands of people whose thoughts are with you now.

You have gained the respect and admiration of the world by your attitude in victory and you have also kept that respect by the manner in which you accepted that bolt out of the blue yesterday.

It is one thing to be able to accept success. It is far harder to take defeat, especially when it comes the way it did. Your friends still feel the same way they always felt. The others don't matter – they never did, really. You have probably gained more friends and admirers by the way you accepted this defeat. The quiet way you carried yourself off the Centre Court, even though your heart must have been breaking, will have gained you untold wealth in new friends and admirers.

I say to you don't let it get you down, as I'm sure you won't. There is always another day and at the age of nineteen, with a tennis game such as yours to back you up, the good days will far outnumber the bad.

Yours sincerely
Fred Perry'

Even though she would go on to take the title three times, Wimbledon would always remain her bogey tournament all throughout her career. Had she recognised the negativity of the press lead up in those first years she would never have paid any heed to it. She, of all people knows how Ivan Lendl must feel every time he goes to Wimbledon. Her curse has seemingly transferred to his head! She reset her sights, put the loss behind her, learning from its painful lesson.

Her twentieth birthday was spent aboard the majestic QE2 liner cruising its way across the Atlantic to the USA: the country in which she felt very much at home. Most of her finest tennis was played here, for she felt that American crowds appreciated the effort, diligence and determination it took to become the world's top player.

Back home in Australia she always felt the crowds never supported her as she was generally the number one seed and rarely the underdog. The Australian crowds always seemed to support the underdog – regardless of what country they came from. Perhaps it was a throw back of a negative self-image of a country born with the 'rejects and rabble' of English society. It was a 'them' and 'us' mentality and as she had become a tall poppy in Australian society, she was always open to having her stem cut out from under her.

Americans applauded and enthusiastically voiced their approval; they became part of the match! Australian crowds were there merely to spectate, to see a show just like a Melbourne Cup outing; only the players replaced the horses. Likewise in England the players' skills and talents were often secondary to the attendance of Royalty, the latest fashions and the chance to be seen consuming vast quantities of 'strawberries and cream'.

So, arriving in America she felt renewed, confident and totally at peace. She had a new goal; to prove she deserved the number one world ranking, despite her Wimbledon defeat. In front of fifteen thousand people at Forest Hills she played Maria Bueno in the semi-final. She knew the crowd were not behind her that day for the Americans loved the graceful Brazilian. But despite the parochial support, Margaret was able to play both the crowd and Maria, to win her way into her first ever US Open title. She met Darlene Hard, the current title holder, in the final. Darlene had been in Sydney earlier that year and had been beaten by Margaret and had vowed to avenge that defeat when she got Margaret on her home turf. Now she had her chance, but Margaret's grim determination not to lose this one – for if she won she would be the first Australian to win the US Open – was something Darlene hadn't counted on. Also if she won it would partially compensate her Wimbledon loss and prove she could compete in the big matches. And a big match it was, as Margaret outplayed and outlasted the aggressive Hard to take the match in three sets. She was delighted but once again she could see Mr Rutter shaking his head and saying – 'You have to win in straight sets if you want to win Wimbledon!'

She returned home to Australia in 1962 to a hero's welcome and was dutifully awarded a civic reception; the whole of Albury turned out to welcome their famous daughter home. She had won three out of the four Grand Slam tournaments – only Wimbledon had escaped her net. It was a superb climax to the year as she was also the first Australian to win at Rome, Paris and Forest Hills. She often wondered how the official who wished her all the ill-luck in the world felt; it was obvious his prayers were not being answered.

Wimbledon did not elude her for long. In fact the very next year an elated Margaret Smith won the coveted title for the first time and became the first Australian to do so! She beat Billie Jean King in two straight sets. Now she could see a smiling Mr Rutter – 'See I told you you'd only win if you won in straight sets!'

The next year 1964, she lost her title to Maria Bueno and then regained it from her the following year, 1965. The only title to elude Margaret and stop her from completing a Grand Slam in 1965, was the French Open in which she was the runner up!

In 1966 she again tried to take a third Wimbledon Crown after having won her seventh Australian title in succession. However she was not successful going out in the semi-finals. She then made a startling decision to retire; in hindsight a little premature for she was only twenty-four years of age, and her best tennis was still ahead of her in terms of experience, strength and temperament.

She had had enough. Her heart was not in it anymore and she felt it was time to do something other than play tennis for a time. She had lost her vision, she had no new goals and she was perishing in a sea of doubt as to why she was playing anymore. Her mother would be delighted.

Margaret always believed she would retire from the sport when she began to lose more than she won; that had started in 1966 and culminated with her shock semi-final loss to Billie Jean.

She was bored with tennis; it had become robotic

and stale. The constant grind of travel, different hotels, never-ending practise sessions and pressure of championship matches had taken its toll. Tennis no longer stimulated her sense of challenge for she had captured every crown she had gone after.

Perth was the city to which she retired. It was isolated and had a tremendous climate, thus she could live here in relative obscurity and avoid the glare of publicity which always surrounded her.

Even at twenty-four she had never shaken off her shy, gawky, country girl image – at least in her own mind. Interviews and public speaking were the last thing she ever wanted to do. What often was labelled in her as arrogance, was nothing more than an acute case of shyness.

In Perth she moved in with a well known sporting family the Plaisteds; having become a close friend of Helen Plaisted as a teenager in Melbourne. Helen was also on the tennis circuit being one of WA's leading tennis players. Helen and Margaret had often spoken about setting themselves up in a sporting clothes business once their tennis days were behind them. Now the two young hopefuls established a business in a ritzy Perth suburb of Claremont and called it the Peep Hole. Another friend Anne Edgar, a physical education teacher joined the two of them, and they all eventually moved into a large Claremont house which Margaret had purchased for $10,000 – the amount she had accumulated in her six years on the amateur circuit. For the first time in her life Margaret had lots of dates and went to parties;

drank beer and danced many a night away. Tennis seldom crossed her mind and no one reminded her of it. That was just the way she liked it.

She first met Barry Court, her future husband, as part of a group of friends who were constantly together. Barry had invited her to his Yacht club dance. She hadn't really wanted to go but was finally coerced into it by Barry's insistence that she go out with him.

She soon learnt Barry didn't take no for an answer that night or any other night. He was fun loving and adventurous and loved the water as she did. They made an outstanding couple as Barry's six foot two frame stood head and shoulders over her; one of the rare individuals who did.

Barry brought her out of her shyness and introversion, for he had all the happy-go-lucky ways of a true extrovert. His gregarious father Sir Charles Court, had an exuberance for life and an ageless vitality, despite his fifty odd years, that saw him remain as Premier of Western Australia for a record twenty years. His mother Lady Court was a down-to-earth woman who took everyone on face value; she was never impressed by who someone was supposed to be. When meeting Margaret for the first time she warmly welcomed her into her home and asked her whether she knew that she had the same name as that famous tennis player.

Within six months the couple were married. With marriage came a new perspective. Margaret wanted Barry to meet the friends she had made all over the world and to see the places and to experience the life she had led as a professional tennis player.

It was decided that they would go away as a type of honeymoon with Margaret playing the odd tournament or two as they travelled. Now she was enthused once again. She knew that having Barry beside her would solve most of those lonely lost feelings that she had encountered when travelling alone on the circuit. Now she had someone special who would be 100% behind her. She intended to only go for the year and then go touring but her sensational comeback changed all those plans.

During her fourteen months away she had put on weight but still had a good relative standard of fitness because she had taken up squash and was the Western Australian number two player behind Helen Plaisted – now Helen Muir – who was the current number one. Brian Bowman, a Perth businessman and a top tennis player in Perth, helped her by hitting regularly with her. It took hard work and diligence but Margaret got back into it with a renewed vigour; now she had someone she loved to show how well she could play tennis.

Barry was a tremendous help as they decided to go abroad after she made the final of the Australian Open in Melbourne in 1968. He became adept at booking hotels, plane reservations and handling luggage; all the things Margaret was glad to abandon. It left her totally free to concentrate on tennis.

By the time she was due to play in England after touring South Africa, tennis had gone Open and amateurism was dead. It was a happy coincidence, for in that year she would go on to make more money than all the previous years combined.

Her comeback year proved promising and with her win in the first truly Open Australian in 1969 she decided to tour again, for the first leg of the Grand Slam was already hers. Right on target she won the French Open for the third time and then set herself for Wimbledon. But once again she was thwarted by her jinxed tournament. An incredibly fit and powerful Anne Jones would beat her in the semi-finals and would go on to win the 1969 Wimbledon title, becoming the first English player – man or woman – to do so since 1961.

Immediately afterwards, Margaret would once again avenge that devastating loss to go on and take the US Open, giving three out of the four Grand Slam events. She was frustrated at having come so close once again and set her sights so that nothing was going to stop her from taking it the very next year. Margaret had the fire back in her belly; she knew the Slam was there; she hoped it would only take one more year.

And that is exactly what happened. 1970 would be the greatest year of her tennis career. She was about to achieve the one goal that had so far eluded being added to her impressive list of victories. The record books for the Australian Open were being rewritten as Margaret captured her ninth Australian title to set herself off on the first leg of the Slam.

Next was the French Championship. It was so

important, that Margaret flew to Los Angeles for a week of secret coaching to straighten out some hitting problems she was experiencing. It paid off as her confidence was restored, and she cruised to take her fourth French title.

Now she had two of the four under her belt but she remained cautiously optimistic for she had been here three times before in 1962, 1964 and 1969. She went into the Wimbledon tournament as the number one seed after winning the Queens tournament – the curtain raiser for Wimbledon – and with her old rival Billie Jean as the number two. If they both played true to form they were seeded to meet in the final.

And true to their seedings they did meet in the final. It was a battle of the heavyweights of tennis. Neither player was totally fit, Margaret had a badly injured left ankle and Billie Jean supported a knee bandage. But despite their injuries the two fought the longest tennis game in Wimbledon history lasting two hours and twenty seven minutes.

It was a match of equals; both players had the iron will and determination that made them both champions. But only one could win and truly be called the number one in the world this day. Margaret was determined it was to be her; but so was the gutsy Billie Jean.

Margaret had disliked playing Billie Jean for she found her constant verbal retorts very off-putting. This was Billie's form of gamesmanship that had crept into the game and Margaret didn't like it. However she had always respected the great talent of

Billie Jean which was obviously mutual, for when Billie Jean was asked who she hated to play and why she had replied 'Chris Evert and Margaret Court – just because they were who they were'.

Sparks flew on the centre court. It was like the showdown at the OK Corral as the big guns of tennis fired their best shots at each other. The first set lasted a full hour and a half with Margaret finally taking it 14/12 – there being no tie breaker operating then. Another hour would pass before she would finally throw off the Wimbledon jinx of centre court nerves in this pressure match to take the second set 11/9 and her third Wimbledon title. It was also the third leg of the Grand Slam now tucked under her belt. All that remained was the US Open, her favourite tournament and which was only two months away.

The press, once derogatory, now headlined her amazing performance. The tennis public hailed Margaret Court as the 'Queen of Queens.'

Her ankle injury had still not healed going into the US Open, and her doctors advised her to withdraw or risk permanent injury. But Margaret was not about to let a sore foot rob her of her long-awaited goal.

Luckily she advanced easily through to the final without further mishap but the mental pressure became horrific. She was within one match of the long awaited Slam and no-one was about to let her forget it.

Rosie Casals was the other finalist that day but all interest centred on whether Margaret Court would take the Slam that day after her ten year endeavour. Casals seemed set to cause an upset when, with the Americans obviously behind her as their compatriot, she played extremely well to equalise the game by winning the second set 6/2 after Margaret had taken the first 6/2.

But Margaret steadied, tightened up her concentration and prayed for help. This was the most crucial set of her life. She remembered the pain of earlier losses at Wimbledon and she was not about to leave this court the same dejected way. She would leave a winner; she didn't care how long she had to play to do it. As it turned out it didn't take long, as she powered her way through the third set winning it 6/1 to take the US Open and her long awaited Grand Slam.

Margaret had finally fulfilled her desire to return to be the number one and win the Grand Slam. Her wins encouraged her to keep playing and she and Barry decided to tour again in 1971. In her usual style, she started the year with a win in the 1971 Australian Open. But her hopes for a Slam were dashed as she failed to win the French Open. Next was Wimbledon, but with the Grand Slam no longer possible, the motivation had partly gone.

Margaret played well to reach the finals, being in quest of her fourth title. Her opponent was another Australian, Evonne Goolagong. But in this final Margaret would be completely off her game. Her co-ordination and timing was so bad that she stood at the net and let balls that she would volley away for winners, go straight over her head to land comfortably in by at least two feet! She herself went 'walkabout' – the trait so often attributed to her opponent Evonne who is of Aboriginal descent – in this important final.

Evonne had not faced her idol at her best this day, for she knew Margaret was clearly not her usual powerful self. But to her credit she richly deserved her popular win by cleverly exploiting this inability of Margaret to serve and volley effectively. Margaret, although unhappy at losing in such a bewildering manner was happy to see the cheerful face of Evonne receive the coveted Wimbledon trophy in this all Australian final. Evonne had always been a fair competitor and everyone loved this simple unassuming girl from the Australian bush.

For weeks before this match Margaret had often complained to Barry that her beer had tasted bitter for she often enjoyed a few cans of Fosters after her matches. Feeling very nauseated and off balance, a trip to the doctor would confirm what she had begun to suspect: that she was indeed three and a half months pregnant.

It was a happy occasion even though it came at an inopportune time, but it was also sad. For Margaret's mother had died ten days before she knew her daughter was pregnant. Margaret withdrew from the US Open and she and Barry went home to Perth to await the birth of their child. Daniel arrived in March 1972. This was something special, so new, but Margaret was not yet ready to swap her tennis racquets for domestic life. She hadn't finished; she knew she had more to give and now she had a new vision. She wanted to be the first mother to become the world's number one. There was another fire burning in her belly.

Chapter 3

Margaret's first major result in her relentless come-back trail was a semi-final berth in the 1972 US Open, six months after she had given birth to Daniel. Now she had her sights set on another possible Grand Slam in 1973 which would automatically place her as the undisputed number 1 and achieve her aim of being the world's first professional tennis mum!

Her win in the 1973 Australian Open, her 11th title, followed by the capture of the French Crown, put her well on the way to achieving the Grand Slam once again. But as always she was cautious, for her infamous bogey tournament, Wimbledon, was still ahead. And once again it would prove to be just as she believed, not her happiest playing ground, for another future champion, a young and talented Chris Evert, would put Margaret out in the semi-final! And to prove it was more a nervous, ingrained stigma than pure playing brilliance, Margaret would bounce straight back to take the US Open to win three out of the four Grand Slam events for 1973. She had achieved her goal of becoming the world's first tennis playing mother in less than a full year after her baby's birth! It was a great statement of her strength and resilience to come back at a time when 'mothers' were thought to be better off at home. She also proved that there is life after pregnancy!

Motherhood seemed to agree with Margaret as she began to play a more relaxed and confident style of tennis. She was content to take things as they came and found that she did not get upset as easily as she had previously.

In light of her 1973 achievements, 1974 promised to be the year that she would totally dominate tennis. She was playing confident, bold tennis – she had at last learned to always play her powerful serve and volley game, in light of the most disappointing match she ever played.

In a 1973 challenge match which was televised to millions throughout the world, she lost to the ageing fifty-five year old, former Wimbledon Mens's champion, Bobby Riggs. It didn't matter in terms of seedings, but in terms of pride, she was devastated. He had so belittled women's tennis, and Margaret felt she needed to stop him dead in his tracks. She felt women's tennis should not be judged according to men's standards. She was no real feminist defender either, preferring to leave politics out of tennis. It was more because he irritated her immensely that she accepted.

Little thought and preparation went into her lead-up to the game as she believed him to be an ageing has-been who couldn't hit the ball hard. But she was not prepared for the shrewd gamesmanship he would use against her. And true to his showman image, his tactics did totally destroy the confidence she had felt, going into the match. Her own pre-match morning was spent fishing the only pair of tennis shoes she had brought with her, from the toilet bowl into which they had been carefully placed by her toddler, Daniel. Getting them dry took the remainder of the morning. She was unaware that this Sunday was actually 'Mother's Day' in America, until she turned up at the San Diego court.

There, with all the flamboyance of a theatrical performance, Bobby Riggs presented her, 'the nicest mother in the game', with a lovely bunch of red roses. The red was appropriate as Margaret was literally seething under this patronising performance. Cameras, as numerous as people, were dotted all around the San Diego playing centre. This unexpected media attention (all invited by Riggs), was also upsetting her because it was now more than just a personal score to settle – fought out in an out of the way court. This game had attracted international media attention.

Now she carried the expectations of millions of women all over the world who hoped she would put the loud chauvinist in his place. She realised they would all be watching. And as usual, once she became nervous she rarely played her powerful dominating game. It was universally recognised that she was undoubtedly the strongest and best all-round player ever to take the court, but she was not the best 'match' player in these highly tense situations. Riggs knew this tension to be her 'achilles heel' and he took full advantage. She tightened up to such an extent, she had trouble remembering anything about the game. Riggs totally swamped her in two straight sets 6/2, 6/1, and happily pocketed the winner-take-all prize money. Margaret was thankful that it had been so quick.

Why she didn't play her own game that day, she just didn't know. But one thing she did know was that she would never again go out and start potting the ball around as she had against Riggs. Her game was to go out and hit with all the power and strength she had acquired and then no-one would beat her like this again. And true to her word she saw out the rest of the 1973 season in dominating form that cemented her further as the world's top player.

1973 was also a time of great change for Margaret in her own personal life. Earlier that year she had been to a church service in Paris, during the French Open, and vividly recalls sitting in the service thinking there had to be more to knowing God than simply being in church.

She had no reality of God as being real or personal to her. He was somewhere up there. She felt like a dried up river bed. There was no flow of life within her. She sat and prayed that day, that God would reveal himself to her in some tangible way. In a way that she could really know that He was really there for her.

The answer to that prayer came later that year

when she was given a book to read by a friend in the US, entitled *How To Be Born Again*. Previously, any religious books given to her had always ended up in the trash can. For some reason she kept this little book, and found herself reading it again and again. Although she did not fully understand the contents, there was something different about this book.

On her return to Perth, in late 1973, she was amazed to hear from her close friend Anne, that she had become a 'born again' Christian. The change in Anne was as dramatic as anything Margaret had ever witnessed. Anne was simply radiant and spiritually buoyant on the inside, something that Margaret wasn't. So it was not long before Margaret accompanied Anne to a similar charismatic pentecostal meeting, where Anne had been so obviously transformed.

At the end of the meeting Margaret responded to the altar call. A man of God challenged all those there, whether they really knew Jesus in a truly personal way as Lord and Saviour. If they did not, they were encouraged to publicly come forward and declare Him to be the Lord of their life. A struggle of infinite proportions went on inside Margaret that night, for she knew that everyone in that meeting would know who she was if she went forward. She was still the world's number one tennis player at that time and her pride in that and being a Catholic all her life, almost stopped her going forward. But she was compelled to go out and give her life to Christ; something she knew she had never done before.

It felt as though someone had switched the light on inside. An incredible peace and joy flooded her whole being. She no longer had any doubts as to the tangibility of God. He was as real to her as anything she had perceived with her natural senses. He was now so close, that the moment of being 'born again' of the Spirit of God is forever etched into her memory, as the greatest day of her whole life.

Nothing could compare to this wonderful feeling and nothing could take it away from her.

Margaret continued to play tennis right through the rest of 1973, all the time knowing that Jesus was with her. At all times she shared her experience with those who asked her and was content to steadily grow in the things of God. But in December 1973 she found out she was pregnant again, and decided against playing until after the birth of her second child. She and Barry and young Daniel went home to Perth to await the arrival of the baby. They were delighted in her second pregnancy although she felt they could have timed it a little better. She had a great belief that children came as gifts from God – it was more His timing than their timing. It was a wonder that she didn't have a lot more children with an attitude like that!

Little Marika, her first daughter was born after a complicated delivery in July 1974. After some worrying days with Marika in intensive care, Margaret was able to take home the new addition to the Court household.

There she became an ordinary wife and mother

with the same everyday chores and pressing problems as every other housewife. Tennis seemed a long way away, but she was still making decisions inside. Could she make it back again? Was she too old at thirty three?

She really didn't know what to do, and while she stayed at home being mum, she enjoyed the company of her two closest friends Helen and Anne who had young children of their own.

Eventually Margaret made the decision to return to tennis, for she felt she still had more to offer. She had been in the prime of her career when Marika was born and she felt strong enough to cope with the rigours of tough tournament play despite being the mother of two young children: one only months old!

In late 1974 she decided to 'test the waters' by playing in South Africa before making the final decision to tour once again as a professional. Her form was promising and although she did not win the open singles, that honour going to Kerry Melville of Australia, she teamed with her young protegé Di Fromholtz to finish as runner-up in the doubles. She did however, go home a winner of the mixed doubles. Since she had acquitted herself well considering the shortness of her preparation, she and Barry decided to tour once more in 1975 taking both children and a nanny along with them.

Her return in early 1975 to play the Australian Open was not as easy as her first comeback. She was now thirty-three years of age and the demands of childbirth had taken its toll on her ligament elasticity and general muscle strength. She called upon the wizardry of Stan Nicholes in Melbourne to help prepare her for the rigours of tournament play. She was merciless in her preparation; driven by a new goal to make a successful comeback for the second time. She ran, jogged and lifted weights, and although not extremely confident she entered the Australian Open even though she had not competed in a grand slam event for over a year.

Unfortunately her progress was halted as she went out in the quarter finals; an amazing feat just to get there, to a young teenager, Martina Navratilova from Czechoslovakia. After the game Margaret prophetically predicted that she felt Martina would one day be the top player in the world. She could see in Martina the same raw talent, courage and sheer determination which had always characterised her own game. She sensed a new breed of tennis champions had been birthed with Martina, and others like Chris Evert and Evonne Goolagong, who were making their presence felt in the same way as she, Billie Jean and Maria Bueno had done. It was inevitable that these youngsters who idolised and modelled their game on hers would one day beat her, playing just like she did.

Despite the defeat Margaret felt she was playing reasonably enough to go overseas once again on the professional circuit. At times she began to question what she was really doing and why was she doing it. Perhaps it was the money that she was now earning and could still earn before she retired that was her motivation. Obviously it counted but it was some-thing within her that had not been truly solved.

An incredible confusion would start to emerge in her as she couldn't seem to equate her new Chris-tianity with her old aggressive style of play. She believed that to win she had to be aggressive, tough and relentless; attributes she felt couldn't be recon-ciled with more godlike qualities. But this tour seemed to be more fun than before as she enjoyed having her family alongside her. It was at Wimbledon that year when she made a private decision to retire at the end of the year after fulfilling all her scheduled commitments for the year.

Margaret had always recognised that deep within her she had some purpose that was to be fulfilled, and she knew it was no longer tennis. She was about to take a new step into a totally different life that not even she could have anticipated.

God was calling, and she had an incredible thirst to know more about her Christian conversion. The little she did know she had shared willingly throughout the tour with those who had asked her. Sharing Jesus with them really excited her in much the same way as tennis had done in her early life.

Her priorities had definitely shifted. She recog-nised that the transition had come because she could no longer visualise her goals, for they were no longer centred around tennis. In many ways it was this ability that had taken her from the realm of the mediocre player to the brilliant heights of a cham-pion. The world had seen the last of the best of her tennis – not because she was not capable of reproducing it – she simply had no desire to do so anymore. Her extraordinary love affair with the game would never be over; it would always be there with her. But this time there would be no going back. That door was finally closed as a new one was about to open!

On her return to Perth with her family she began to devote more of her time to finding out more about the reality of Jesus within her. There was so much she didn't understand, for so many things were incomprehensible to her. She didn't understand how a God of love seemed to allow so much sickness, suffering and disease in the world. She herself had just suffered a miscarriage and had believed it was God's will that she lose the child. A dilemma of immense proportions was beginning to develop.

Her heart was zealous for God but it had long been blinded by religious traditions which made the religious way of life; the deeds, penances and good works more important than the simple truth of the written word of God which glorifies Jesus alone.

My first coach Wal Rutter takes a junior clinic in Albury

With Rod Laver after we had each won the Victorian singles
championship 1962

Sir Norman Brookes, Australia's first Wimbledon champion (1907), and
Australia's first woman champion (1963)

Wedding to Barry Court (1967)

September 14, 1970, I was the women's champion of England, Australia,
France, and the United States

Ladies Singles Champion Wimbledon (1970)

Rhema Bible Training Centre Graduation 1983 with Sir Charles Court

A flower bouquet presented by a grateful listener after Bible teaching

Ministering to the sick

A family holiday in Monte Carlo

Margaret and Barry on their sheep farm showing stud Merinoes for sale

A recent photo of Margaret and Barry

Margaret by commemorative statue unveiled in her honour, Melbourne,
Australia Day, January 1993.

Chapter Four

Margaret retired officially in the latter part of 1975, but still competed until all her pledged appearances in events, such as the Women's Virginia Slims Tours, were completed in the first part of 1976. Once she had fulfilled these US commitments, she, Barry and the two children returned to Australia; to set up home in Perth. They moved into their stately old home, purchased two years before, in Claremont. Margaret was truly excited at the prospect of doing further renovations to make the old residence a real family home. Of course it already had a tennis court; they would not have bought it otherwise.

Tennis was not totally forgotten as Margaret still kept in masterly touch by coaching on the family court. In many ways, she did not really want to coach, preferring to hang her racquet up for good since she had retired. But she could not escape the feeling that she had so much to offer and needed to use that gift.

'I never accepted any money for the coaching I did' she admits. 'I just wanted to help anyone who showed some promise how to develop their game, and how they should structure their training routines to achieve their aims. I never forgot the wonderful start I had, which would never have been possible without the free coaching sessions I received. In some ways this was a way I could repay that debt.'

Her coaching sessions soon moved from the Claremont address as she and Barry decided to purchase a wonderful Nedlands home, high on the hill overlooking the beautiful Swan River and which had panoramic views over the city of Perth. It was an idyllic setting considering Barry's love of yachting and her love of the river. They also had lots of room at the bottom of the block to build an enormous tennis court fully equipped with night lights, to cater for the proposed social nights of tennis they would have.

Her life was now very full as she became pregnant once more and gave birth to her third child and second daughter Teresa, in November 1977. At this time too, Barry was very involved in the running of the family property, near the picturesque town of New Norcia, two hours drive to the northeast of Perth. Sheep and wheat were the mainstay of produce on their large holding of five thousand acres. This left Margaret quite a lot on her own, supervising the three children when Barry was not there. Although they had a full-time manager, Barry was highly involved in the overall management of the farm. Farming had always been something he had desired to do, having earned his woolclassing qualification with the pastoralist company 'Elders', many years before Margaret had actually met him.

Margaret and Barry had always thought that when she retired they would actually go farming. They both loved the outdoor life. Whenever Margaret was at home on holidays, taking a break from her hectic tennis commitments, the farm had always provided a perfect retreat.

As busy as she was being a wife, mother and coach Margaret still found time to attend various meetings concerned with the growth of her Christian faith. She had a compulsive, driving desire in her heart to know more about the spiritual aspect of her life. Along with a group of friends she attended as many meetings as was humanly possible. She could not stop thinking about the call that she knew was on her life, which had been there from the day she asked Jesus into her life.

'I just wanted everyone to know about Jesus; it was that simple' she recalls. 'I needed to know a lot more myself, for there were many questions that I knew I could not answer. But I did know one thing for certain, and that was that Jesus was alive and so very real to me. If I died at that moment I knew I would go to be with Him.'

Barry was a tower of strength at this time and although heavily involved in farming he willingly assumed the role of babysitter as Margaret pursued her search, wanting so much to grow in the things of God.

Unfortunately for her, the meetings she attended often centred around a practice known as 'inner healing'. She was taught that she needed to go back into her past life and uncover any suppressed memories of people and experiences that may have adversely affected her. She was further told that if these things weren't worked through and eradicated from her memory then she would never be truly free and spiritually mature.

Had she known the scripture in 2 Corinthians 5:17

> *'If any man be in Christ he is a new creature: old things are passed away; behold all things are become new,'*

her life would have taken a different direction, but she did not, for she had no knowledge of the Scriptures, not having been brought up with them. She would have avoided a lot of the heartache and pain she encountered as she tried to dig up the skeletons of her past and attach some deep, meaningful significance to them. She sensed that looking back was not the way to go to find the answers she needed. One thing she had learned as an athlete, was to always put the games already played behind and concentrate on the game ahead. True, she had learnt many a valuable lesson from an analysis of the game, but to dwell there would mean certain defeat in the future.

'I became totally self-centred with all this emphasis on looking in at myself. I was not really aware of my family either, almost to the point of neglect, as I consistently analysed my life to see why I felt so guilty, unworthy, fearful and totally insignificant. My self-esteem crumbled under this type of scrutiny. I truly did not even feel human any more as I wept and cried perpetually in a state of emotional distress. I had nothing to anchor my hope on and floated about in a sea of bewilderment until I was nothing more than a shipwrecked shell.'

There was not a lot of sound biblical teaching at this time, and Margaret found herself hearing things from a variety of speakers but nothing from anyone who had a solid knowledge of the word of God. She had never heard that God and His word are one, something she desperately needed to hear, for without this stability of God's unchanging word, she had no real basis for any concrete change.

The more she went into inner healing the more confused she became, for there was not a great deal of 'past' for her to dig through to find the reason for her enormous feelings of inferiority and worthlessness. She had always lived a good, moral life before God and wherever she was in the world playing tennis, she would go to church on Sunday if possible.

Margaret knew that she had never been really loved as a young child. Her mother, although loving, had allowed a certain amount of fear to override her ability to love freely and her father, like most Australian men of the post-war era, had found it difficult to show any real display of affection to his youngest daughter.

But none of those experiences were the cause of her own mammoth fear and insecurity developing, although she admits they contributed. The problem was not that she had these insecurities, but how she was to be rid of them in her life. Looking back all the time, only kept her mind centred on the problems until they became like a stronghold over her mind. There seemed to be no future ahead; living for today was impossible, as the past was always uppermost in her thoughts. The more she tried to forget it, the more her mind bombarded her with a confused tangle of mixed emotions.

Even the normal pride she had in being the world's best tennis player was now seen to be an evil thing in her life and one she needed to deal with. It was labelled an evil spirit that needed to be cast out of her. This wrong emphasis only magnified the fear, for now she had things to deal with she had never considered before.

She began to think that she needed to be set free from any thing that was remotely detected to be an ungodly part of her life. This went on for a period of time and it really only increased her fears enormously, for now she felt she was in the grip of Satan himself.

Confusion, disappointment and self-hatred took a mighty hold on her life. Fear opened the door to physical illness. Her once powerful, muscular frame became terribly emaciated. The lack of peace, her confused thoughts and resulting emotional instability would all take their toll.

'I listened to man, I followed man and I trusted man and did not look to the truth of the Scriptures myself. I thought that God was a God of judgement and so I prayed for God to break my heart. I felt that

He was out to get me, and so I was hitting myself over the head all the time, and I didn't even know it!'

A torn valve of the heart came as the answer to her 'prayer' to be broken. She felt totally confused; wondering just what she had done to deserve such a painful answer. Immediately she was put onto heart tablets with a specialist diagnosis that she would be on them for the rest of her life. She felt hurt, lonely and depressed, and could not see any way out of the dark pit she was in. She did not really know just where she would actually end up. There were very few people to whom she could turn for help. Not even Barry, who was always loving and supportive, really understood the full depths of the despair she felt.

Thankfully she had Anne and Helen, her two closest friends who did understand and became pillars of support to her. They would often come over and spend the night with Margaret when Barry was away at the farm. She was terrified of being alone during the night, for she felt a presence of evil around her that was so real that she could almost 'see' grotesque faces laughing at her. Both friends would sit and pray with her, sometimes all through the night, reassuring her that everything would be just fine.

The 'deliverance' team assigned to her, had put so much emphasis on there being a demonic spirit behind every single ailment or feeling, that it had made her more fearful than she had ever been before. She was 'delivered' of spirits of nausea, fear, cramp, insomnia, pride ... the list was endless as every time she went to seek help she was relieved of another demon or two! Utter confusion and turmoil reigned in her life because she suspected that she had no demons to be rid of in the first place. She was at a dangerous spiritual place – the evil things of the spirit dreadfully real, without the counterbalance of the integrity of the word of God, which shows the defeat of the forces of darkness and renders them totally harmless to knowledgeable believers. This type of 'deliverance ministry', was something she finally decided to have nothing more to do with.

Barry did not understand the spiritual torment she was going through and really wanted nothing to do with anything so radical. All he could see was that it had reduced his once outgoing wife to a complete emotional mess, crippled with fear, too afraid to live life and enjoy it as she had always done before.

There was such fear and torment in her life, that even to this day, she remembers its awesome power. At times she felt it was like a type of paralysis, leaving her unable to perform the simple, mundane functions of her own household. Her mind was like a windmill, turning over and over, with confused and fearful thoughts flooding her head incessantly. Sleep was only possible with the help of sleeping tablets; her mind just could not stop ticking over. Insomnia became a way of life and soon severe depression descended over her life like a large, black storm cloud. 'When morning came I wished it was night and when night came I wished it was morning. I had no peace, either awake or fitfully asleep; it didn't matter. I really thought that if it was going to be like this on earth then I would rather go home and be with God. I was of no use to anybody; not to myself, my family or even to God.' Being told all the arguments, however logical and rational, that such terror was unwarranted because she had so much to live for, with a devoted husband and family and enough wealth accumulated for the remainder of her life, did not ease the situation at all. In fact, it only produced further guilt, as she knew there was no reason for her to feel the way she did – but she did!

Margaret felt like she was in another world. She could not see her way out of the mess she was in. To turn to the pastors was unthinkable, because she knew that she would only be subjected to further spirits being cast out of her!

In 1979 she was hospitalised and treated for a variety of symptoms. This enforced stay gave her time to think and question the direction of her life. It had not got any better, but far worse. She knew this should not be so! Somehow she sensed that she had been involved in things that were not quite right and for the time being decided to put everything on hold. She wanted nothing more to do with any of it.

Chapter Five

The turning point would come in her life not long after she came out of hospital. Two business men told Margaret of a powerful, faith-teaching video they had seen, featuring a prominent pastor from America, Fred Price. Margaret remembered that as a new Christian, she had been invited to give her testimony at a Full Gospel Men's fellowship in Hawaii. She had refused, a little fearful of public speaking, until she found out that Fred Price was going to be the guest speaker. She had heard some wonderful things about his ministry back home in Australia and really wanted to hear him speak.

In that meeting, Fred Price acting on a word of knowledge, prophesied that God was healing someone in the audience of stomach ulcers at the very time he was speaking. That someone was Barry, who told Margaret the good news of his healing some hours later. To Margaret it was very good news, for it meant she would no longer have to be careful about the type of food she served Barry; he could eat anything. The only thing that disappointed her about the healing was that she thought Barry would be so excited that he would give his life to Christ immediately. But he did not. She had experienced a scriptural truth that Jesus had often taught, that seeing, or even experiencing a miracle, would not necessarily make a believer of anyone; it was always by faith. Obviously, Barry was not yet at that faith level.

But what really excited her was the fact that this video had been brought to her attention by these two men, who had no idea that she had already seen and heard this man and had been very impressed by his faith message, even then.

As she sat and watched the video (the first thing she had even attempted to touch with a 'Christian' message for months), she felt as though she was hearing something positive and uplifting for the very first time. She knew that she had been exposed to his dynamic teaching back in Hawaii, all those years ago, but she obviously had not been ready to absorb it. It felt as though a light switch had been turned on inside her. She heard for the very first time that the word of God was the only way to grow in faith and to overcome any area of defeat in her life. She sat transfixed, took pages of notes and studied the scriptures he gave.

In 1979, Margaret began to attend a newly formed word church in Perth, which taught along the same lines as Dr Price. The word, as found in the Bible, was its sole reference and foundation. 'If you can't find what I teach you in the Word, then disregard my message', the pastor would tell his congregation. It was here that Margaret learnt that she needed to find scriptures relevant to her needs, and put them into her life to effect change. She sensed that her answers were all tied into really understanding the word she needed. The words she heard were as vital to her as was the discovery by Martin Luther of his life changing scripture ...

> *'The just shall live by faith.'*   (Romans 1:17)

Not only did this scripture turn his whole life around but it affected a whole Church age.

The scripture she found and personalised and spoke over her life was from 2 Timothy 1:7,

> *'For God hath not given **me** the spirit of fear, but of power, and of love and of a sound mind ...'*

and the discovery of this scripture, at that time, would turn her whole life around forever. This was the only scripture she could memorise entirely at that time for her mind was still very confused. Over and over she said it; day and night, night and day. She constantly repeated it when fear, doubt and confusion were trying to take back the small amount of ground they had lost to this positive affirmation, which was beginning to push them from their stronghold over her mind. The more she spoke it, the more her mind began to believe the things she said and slowly it began to act just like it was so.

Somehow, she did not really know how, the fear

started to diminish. Her mind stopped spinning in circles, so that she was able to read and memorise further scriptures. She began to take scriptures as her 'spiritual' medicine, just as she was still taking her physical medicine. She learnt that as she was speaking them over herself daily, she was washing herself in the water of God's word. Slowly, she sensed many other areas of her life changing also, and it was all good.

She listened to lots of other people's testimonies and heard the good news that Jesus had healed and restored them, and made them complete people. She felt that if God had done all that for someone else He would do it for her, for she had found a scriptural truth behind her reasoning

'... *that God is no respecter of persons.'*

(Acts 10:34)

What God did for any one person, He must do for anyone who operates the necessary principles. Margaret had a zealous desire to find out just how these godly principles worked. The testimonies she heard further encouraged her, and for the first time she sensed there was a way out of the mess she was in.

Although she was still physically ill, tired and drained, with a few too many cares and worries, she knew that the fearful torment was no longer there. Over and over again she kept repeating the scripture '... *God has not given me the spirit of fear, but of power, and of love and of a sound mind'*. This was the start of her growth in faith, for she was calling those things that be not as though they are ... and not looking at the natural evidence which was that she had no *'power, love and a sound mind'*.

> *'Faith cometh by hearing, and hearing by the word of God.'* (Romans 10:17)

Since Margaret did nothing else for the next few months of her life it was inevitable that her faith level would grow, for she had at last stumbled on the scriptural formula for the growth in faith that she had always earnestly desired.

> *'Now faith is the substance of things hoped for, the evidence of things not seen.'*
> (Hebrews 11:1)

Her mind stopped going around in confused circles as she began to stabilise her thought life and bring it under the transforming effect of the word. The Bible contained a whole wealth of wisdom on how she could keep her mind centred on God and remain in perfect peace; something she had once thought impossible, but no longer.

Her diligence to train and apply herself to the arduous task of getting her body into the peak of physical condition during her tennis years, would now pay off as she applied this same type of diligence to keeping the word of God – especially the scriptures that had relevant significance to her particular problem – before her eyes and in her mouth at all times.

Nothing could be clearer to her as to why she had suffered so much. She had never read, meditated and attended to the word. She was determined that the word would not escape her attention ever again. It held the key to her salvation, healing, wholeness, soundness and general well-being. It was the sound solid basis on which she had begun to build her faith. The word was to be the 'inner healing' in her life. As she put God's word into the areas of hurt and concern, it drove out all the grief, unforgiveness and brokenheartedness.

Unlike the 'inner healing' practice she first tried, which simply became a pacifier, the word actually dealt with the problem. For the word is health and healing, and it sets you free!

The scripture

> '...I can do all things through Christ which strengtheneth me,' (Philippians 4:13)

was the scripture that she knew she was to base her faith on for the healing she needed in her body. Daily she repeated the scripture over and over to herself, and personalised it to read that ... 'she could do all things through Christ that strengthens her'. The more she said it, the more she started to believe it. The more she said it, the stronger she became. The more she said it, the more her faith began to rise. She also began to add other scriptures relating to healing, to her daily confession.

'But they that wait upon the Lord shall renew their strength; they shall mount up with wings as eagles; they shall run, and not be weary; and they shall walk, and not faint.' (Isaiah 40:31)

The scriptures themselves seemed to have a wonderful healing and soothing effect, even as she spoke them.

The day the full impact of the reality that her faith had grown through hearing and hearing the word of God, was a day forever etched into Margaret's mind. Her close friend Helen, had dropped by to pay Margaret a routine visit as she had regularly done since Margaret had taken ill. She quite innocently remarked that Margaret looked particularly tired on this day.

'No, I can do all things through Christ that strengthens me' Margaret replied, surprising Helen and even herself, with this unusually bold statement. The moment the words left her lips she realised that hope had gone, to be replaced with a confident sense of 'knowing' that she was healthy, even though she still looked and appeared to be very sick. It was at that time, she realised, that the word had become 'flesh' in her. 'I knew from that day forward that I would be totally and perfectly healed; it was only a matter of time.'

That healing was not instant but she began to act like it was. She started to step out and go for light jogs and have a hit of tennis. She began to set her home in order and felt capable of doing more things around the house. At times she felt like throwing away all her medications, but because there was still a remnant of uncertainty there – and she knew it, she kept taking the prescribed drugs for her heart. Her dependence on sleeping tablets and anti-depressants had almost gone.

The change in her appearance and general demeanour was remarkable, especially to those who had watched her slide into the pit of depression. She still had a long way to go, and she jumped at the suggestion that she should go to the newly established Rhema Bible School and study the word in a more official and formalised manner.

Margaret wanted to go desperately, knowing that anyone who desired to go and study God's word was always in His perfect will. Ultimately, it was a decision that depended on Barry's consent, and with a little bit of powerful lobbying she found herself in the class of 1982. The school had a crèche for her two youngest children, Lisa and Teresa. Danny and Marika were now at school. The school ran according to the same schedule as the children's school, so Margaret had the same school holidays. It also only ran from 9 am to 12.30 pm, catering for parents and part time workers alike.

Bible School was a whole new experience for Margaret. Never before had she been so excited about 'study'. The truths she began to learn astounded her. 'It was as though I had been so blind all those years. Scales of doubt, unbelief and fear fell off me as I studied the word of God in an orderly fashion' she relates.

It was in Bible School that she began to understand the incredible power of her words; good or
bad. Faith-filled words were always positive; fear-
filled words were always negative. Without realising
it she had lived for many years under the snare of the
words of her own mouth. Very few positive, uplifting
words had ever left her lips; she had mostly spoken
the same negative words she heard everyone around
her use. The world was saturated in negativity, for
'good news' rarely made the headlines. Another
thing she had started to notice was that anytime she
did read a paper, or listen to a news report, invariably the highlight of the news was someone collaps-
ing and dying of a heart attack. In the past, fear had
always gripped her and spoken to her, saying that she
would be next! She refused to listen to bad news,
realising that what she heard and saw influenced the
way she reacted in her own life. She only wanted to
hear positive and uplifting words.

The word of God, the most positive of all words,
had never been put in front of her like this. She was
excited to find such wisdom in the Bible that
explained so many reasons for her own past defeats.

> *'Death and life are in the power of the tongue:*
> *and they that love it shall eat the fruit thereof.'*
> (Proverbs 18:21)

Up to now her words had created 'death' and not
life. She had constantly spoken about her fears, worries, cares, concerns, illness, guilt, insecurities ... all

very real but all very negative. Immediately she began to turn her words around to the positive; speaking the desired answer by faith. Anytime the negative thoughts came, she did not give them any power by speaking them into existence; instead she thought the exact opposite, for God's word is always the opposite to defeat, despair and discouragement.

Bible School provided her with a wonderful opportunity to grow in the word of God and to feast upon it for three solid hours a day. This 'word diet' was a scriptural principle that was needed for growth. She saw that as her natural physical body had need of food three times a day, so too, did her spirit man have need of food, God's word, at least three times daily.

> *'Man shall not live by bread alone, but by every*
> *word that proceedeth out of the mouth of God.'*
> (Matthew 4:4)

'My people are destroyed for lack of knowledge' (Hosea 4:6), God had told the prophet Hosea many years before. And indeed, it had been this same lack of knowledge that had characterised her own life and seen her defeated. As she studied and learnt the truth of the Scriptures, she felt her mind was being daily loosed from the shackles of confusion that had formerly had it bound.

Healing took on a whole new significance, as she learned that Jesus had died, not only to save her, but to heal her body also. The two separate atonements were provided in His one act on Calvary.

> *'But he was wounded for our transgressions, he*
> *was bruised for our iniquities: the chastisement of*
> *our peace was upon him; and with His stripes we*
> *are healed.'* (Isaiah 53:5)

To learn that Jesus had taken thirty-nine lashes on His back for her every sickness was a great catalyst to her building up her faith to receive her own supernatural healing.

Eight months passed before she underwent a series of tests, initiated by a doctor friend who lives next door, to check out her heart thoroughly. 'You're in perfect health', the report came back. 'The torn valve is totally healed!' Today, ten years later there is still no sign of any heart condition. She is living proof that every scriptural promise that is given in the word of God can come to pass in the life of anyone who will do as she did – believe the promise of God over the reality of the circumstance.

She began to see how her old pre-conceptions of God as a stern, harsh judge, just waiting to catch her out the minute she missed the mark, had distorted her expectation of Him. She always prayed for His help on match days knowing He was out there somewhere; but never really sure that He would answer, for He had a large universe to run and Wimbledon or Forest Hills may not warrant any particular attention that day. If she won, well, that was God's will and if she lost, well, that was God's will too. He was inconsistent in answering some of her more hasty requests thrown up in the midst of the battle. Some of the titles she dearly prayed hardest to win were the very ones she often inexplicably lost. Notwithstanding she was denied a considerable amount of satisfaction and delight, she reasoned that God knew what was best for her, even though losing was not big on her idea of what was her 'best'.

That image of God carried over into her life generally, for as a diligent church-goer all her life she had been indoctrinated with the unscriptural, yet widely preached doctrine, that whatever happened in her life – good or bad – was God's will for her. If she was healthy, well, God be praised; but if she was sick, then God be praised too, for He obviously wanted her sick! Now, she knew once and for all that God wanted His children well.

A time of great strengthening and growth occurred in Margaret, following the supernatural healing of her heart, for she had moved into a higher realm of faith than she had ever known before. She had received earlier healings of a spine curvature and scoliosis, through the scriptural 'laying on of hands' by other believers; but this time her own faith in the written word of God had brought her the healing she desperately needed.

Her faith in the word on salvation, was finally rewarded when Barry gave his life to Christ towards the end of her second year. To have all her family present and saved at the graduation ceremony, was the best graduation she could ever have received. The word had not returned empty when it had been spoken over Barry. God's word never returns to Him without it accomplishing that for which it was sent (Isaiah 55:11).

She graduated in 1983, knowing that ahead was a work to which God had called her, but the time was not yet right. The family took priority over any public ministry for she knew that her 'ministry' for the time being was her husband and children. Her ministry preparation was never neglected however, as she spent the next seven years in various ministries of helps; from nursery to counselling, leading prayer and intercession groups, to hospital and home visitations to the sick. Margaret learnt very early that there can be no victory in any facet of ministry without preceding prayer.

'Prayer is direct communication with God; prayer breaks the powers of darkness; prayer is speaking the word, the answer, into every situation. Prayer changes things.'

Over the years Margaret began to observe that anyone who genuinely knew how to apply faith and the word of God to their problems, always overcame them. Alternatively those who did not, were often miserably defeated. Therefore it was obvious to her (for she too had learnt by experience the same lesson), that it is only the correct application of faith that assures the victory that overcomes the world (1 John 5:4). The next chapter outlines these principles that Margaret, and others, have used to develop their faith to a position of winning faith. These principles to winning faith, do not work for Margaret because she is a famous tennis player, or because

God has seen fit to give her more faith than anyone else. They work because they are all from the word of God. They work for Margaret, in the same way they will for anyone who understands and correctly applies them.

Margaret has no desire to see anyone suffer the way she did for seven years, before learning these principles. No-one need walk in a wilderness of defeat, as she did for the first part of her Christian life, ever again. 'All it takes is one small step of faith in Jesus, to begin the most successful and exciting period of life you can ever experience', she evangelises. 'God's own word says it best.'

> *'I call heaven and earth to record this day against you, that I have set before you life and death, blessing and cursing: therefore choose life, that both thou and thy seed may live.'*
>
> (Deuteronomy 30:19)

Chapter Six

The development of faith begins with a simple life-changing decision. It is clearly laid out that everyone is faced with a choice between life and death; victory or defeat. There is no middle ground. A person can either choose God and therefore life, or he is left with the only alternative, death. The choice is made by accepting Jesus Christ, as Margaret did many years before, or rejecting Him.

Although Margaret had made that all important decision to accept Christ she did not know that this acceptance automatically gave her everything she would ever need for a winning faith to develop. She had not fully understood that the seed of faith had been planted into her own, recreated spirit and that growth would come from watering that seed with the word of God.

Margaret's story dispels the theory that only those who are down and out, with no inner strength of their own seek Christ as a crutch. She accepted Christ when she was number one in the world in tennis; hardly down and out. But it was the lack of knowledge of her righteousness that saw her life degenerate into defeat. To ensure that the people to whom she ministers do not suffer the same defeat she consistently teaches this principle of righteousness as being the foundation to faith.

'Righteousness can be easily understood', she teaches, by giving many practical illustrations. 'My children are my children because they have been born from my body. Nothing can ever destroy that relationship I have with them. They have all the rights and privileges of the Court family. This builds into them a healthy self-esteem and feelings of worth; they know they are valuable and precious to us – everything we have is theirs also. They know that Barry and I would never do anything to hurt them, or reject them, in any way, regardless of what they may do in their lives. God is the same with every single person who is "born" into His family, through accepting the "death" of His son, Jesus Christ. Jesus died so that you could live and He also rose again so that, while you will physically die, you will never spiritually die for He has conquered death, hell and the grave for you. The moment you accept Him in your life,' she explains, 'then you are immediately adopted into God's family as His very own child. All the rights and privileges of God's family – a wonderful heritage – is now yours. God will never do anything to hurt you and certainly will never reject you once you come to Him.'

Understanding this position she had with God, through the new birth, was the key that turned Margaret's life around.

She stresses this principle more than any other she teaches today, for she strongly believes that right-eousness is the foundation to faith and none can have winning faith until they are assured they can go boldly to the throne room of God and find grace and mercy in the time of trouble (Hebrews 4:16). She knows full well, having experienced it herself, that nobody who feels inferior, guilty or worthless will come boldly to God, and God can only work through faith being activated and released.

> *'Faith cometh by hearing, and hearing by the word of God.'* (Romans 10:17)

This scriptural principle is vital to the growth of faith.

No-one had ever told Margaret that her faith could grow and develop by listening to the word of God. She thought that the trials, tests and experiences of everyday life whether good or bad, would determine her faith growth.

Just as Margaret did not become a successful tennis player overnight, so her faith was not per-fected overnight.

Her encouragement to all is always the exhortation to 'read the word, study the word and put that word deep down on the inside of you. Say the word, hear the word and keep on hearing the word.' Her favour-ite scripture is Proverbs 4:20–23:

> *'My son, attend to my words; incline thine ear unto my sayings. Let them not depart from thine eyes; keep them in the midst of thine heart.*

> *For they are life unto those that find them, and health to all their flesh. Keep thy heart with all diligence; for out of it are the issues of life.'*

True scriptural faith, based on the word, has to have corresponding action for it to be effective.

This was a further principle that had helped Margaret receive her healing – healing that had always been available through God's provision, although she had not known how to appropriate it into her life.

'I learned to speak the answer and never the problem. The answer was always a scripture from the word of God, so I found all the scriptures on healing and then personalised them. Day by day as I spoke the words into my body I knew I was not only growing physically much stronger, but my faith for healing was also growing strong. Within months the symptoms began to subside, until finally they left altogether, washed away by the water of God's word.

'The words of your mouth are so powerful,' she consistently emphasises again and again. 'If you have God's word in your heart you will speak faith; if not you will speak fear.'

Looking back to her early tennis career she readily admits that her life had been dominated by fears, cares and worries.

'I often spoke about how I felt and how nervous I was,' she recalls. 'And I always played the way I thought I would. I did not know that even though the negative thoughts had penetrated deep into my heart

I could have aborted them by not speaking them into existence. But instead I birthed them right into exist-ence and gave them power, through my own mouth. I've since learnt that my thoughts, by themselves, have no power, but once I speak them into the atmosphere I have established either a negative or a positive situation; one in which God is able to be involved or one in which the devil is involved.

'God made you in His image and gave you this same ability that He has, to create things with the words of your mouth,' she explains. 'God created the heavens and the earth by the words of His mouth. Your words instantly reveal your inner-most heart beliefs and ultimately will create the world in which you live.'

She firmly believes that too many people speak their problems, instead of speaking the answers. That is what she used to do until she realised that talking about the problem only intensified its hold on her.

'You have to see the answer by faith, before it becomes a reality,' Margaret explains. 'The Holy Spirit is the artist, the word of God the oil, and our spirit man the canvas. The Holy Spirit dips the brush in the oil of the word, and paints it on the canvas of our heart. Through meditation and confession of that word, the picture is painted, until we receive the manifestation of that which we have been believing for. As the Father, Son and Holy Spirit work together, Jesus, the Word, becomes flesh.'

'Faith cometh by hearing, and hearing by the word of God.'   (Romans 10:17)

'There is no other way, there are no shortcuts,' she warns. 'God will reward those who diligently seek Him.'

Margaret Court has never known the meaning of the word quit; it is not a word found in a champion's vocabulary. Winners never quit and quitters never win. She herself has had many bad experiences in her endeavour to grow in her Christian walk, but has never ever given up.

'It is always too soon to quit. Even when it looks like nothing is happening,' she encourages, 'stay with the word. It will work for you; the same as it does for me. God is no respecter of persons. His word is for anyone who will get it, read and study it, speak and confess it, eat it and live it, and base their whole life upon it.

'Faith hears, faith sees, faith speaks, faith acts, and then faith receives. This is always the way it operates,' she explains, 'even in the world system. My success in tennis came by employing these godly principles without even knowing that they were His principles; established for man to be successful in all that he does.

'Frank Sedgeman had told me when I was only twelve years old that he felt I could be the first Australian woman to win Wimbledon. I never forgot those words and deep within me they created a belief that one day it might be a possibility. The more I thought about what I had heard, the more I began to see a vision of myself winning at Wimbledon. A blueprint began to form and I could actually see myself out there, playing and receiving the coveted trophy. Years later I found myself speaking that I *would* be – not *might* be – the first Australian to win Wimbledon. I began to act like it was so; playing with loads of confidence on the way to my goal, surprising everyone except myself, by winning the Australian Open when I was just seventeen.

'The faith I had in my own ability and to realise my ultimate goal of winning Wimbledon was greatly enhanced by this unexpected win. However it would take me another three years to win my first Wimbledon title, despite the fact that I was the top ranked player in the world at that time. The simple truth was I needed those years to build my faith to really believe, and not just hope, I could do it. I finally achieved that aim in 1963. After this Wimbledon victory, my confidence was high and I knew I could win the highly coveted Grand Slam. And that I did in 1970; it was the greatest thrill of my tennis career.

'The principle here, is that what I had faith to achieve, was what I ultimately achieved. Until I really believed I could do it, deep down on the inside of me, I could not do it. In every defeat I suffered, there had always been just enough doubt to allow fear to creep in and overtake me, and rob me of success.' Margaret is quick to show that Jesus had outlined these same principles, many years before, in the gospels. Jesus firstly went about teaching and preaching the good news of the gospel. The people *heard*.

Jesus painted a picture for them of how life could be lived and enjoyed, here on earth. He gave them a blueprint for their lives and put an expectant hope deep into their hearts. The people *saw*.

Jesus then made the people speak back to Him, the faith they had in their hearts. He wanted them to put Him in remembrance of His own words by asking them what they wanted from Him; testing to see if they believed the words He had spoken. And as they affirmed and acknowledged their belief in Him, He was able to move on their faith confession and meet all their expectations. The people *spoke*.

But He always demanded that the faith they had expressed be put into some sort of action.

'Stretch out your hand', He commanded of the man with the withered arm; *'Rise up and walk'*, He instructed the man, lame from birth. *'Go and wash the mud from your eyes'*, He directed the blind man. *'Go and sin no more'* He gently corrected the woman taken in adultery. The people *acted*.

Every time anyone acted on His word, they received their miracle. It was only recorded that in Nazareth, His own home town, He could do no mighty works because of their unbelief. The people *received*.

Margaret teaches these same faith principles as Jesus.

> *'If you can believe, all things are possible to him
> who believes.'* (Mark 9:23, NKJ)

She has a heart to be more and more like Jesus every
day. To have a ministry that is established on the
word of God, and to fulfil the great commission Jesus
gave His body of believers.

> *'Go ye into all the world, and preach the gospel
> to every creature.*
>
> *He that believeth and is baptised shall be
> saved; but he that believeth not shall be damned.*
>
> *And these signs shall follow them that believe;
> In my name shall they cast out devils; they shall
> speak with new tongues; They shall take up ser-
> pents; and if they drink any deadly thing, it shall
> not hurt them; they shall lay hands on the sick,
> and they shall recover.'* (Mark 16:15–18)

She knew the time had finally come in early 1990 to
form her own ministry to fulfil the divine commission
Jesus had given to her.

Barry and the children were totally supportive of
her long awaited move into public ministry. It was
not to be full-time yet, for her two eldest children
were in tertiary studies while the two youngest were
still in secondary school. The Court home still had a
full complement of six, since none had left home and
Margaret knew they still needed a major part of her
time.

Tennis had fallen into the background somewhat

as she had decided not to coach anyone over the last two years, wisely managing the small amount of spare time she had in putting her family first, as she had always done. This she knew was God's order of priority; God first, then family and then ministry. She felt that too many people in ministry had wrongly neglected their families to serve God. Often, this neglect had led to broken family units, with the children blaming God for robbing them of a parent who was never there for them, and so rejecting Him. She did not want to make any such mistake. The coaching had to go since there was simply not enough time in the day to do everything. Ministry preparation and speaking engagements would take up the time she had once spent in coaching tennis.

Chapter Seven

The Ministry

The establishment of Margaret Court Ministries Inc. in early 1991 was the first official step Margaret took to publicly declare the call of God on her life.

She would have been content to serve God in any capacity that He willed but she had no doubt that she was to establish a work under her own name. Accordingly, she established the ministry as a way to achieve the original vision she had been given – to go and proclaim the gospel to all those who needed to hear its good news. All the attributes and the severe disciplines that had contributed to her phenomenal tennis success were about to be put into her own ministry. She knew she would have to be as determined, single minded and dedicated to her ministry calling as she had been in her earlier sporting career, if she was going to fulfil her destiny.

The ministry she established is an outreach ministry to the city of Perth, Western Australia. Halls, community centres and recreational buildings are hired to hold the ministry meetings. Margaret desired to hold her meetings in ordinary, everyday community type buildings, which were non-threatening and easily accessible to the non-churched. Her ministry is not a church and is not meant to take the place of a church. Meetings are held midweek so that the ministry team and the people who come, can attend a regular Sunday service in their own church.

In a desire to operate a ministry that is accountable, Margaret has established a reference board of four pastors from different church affiliations throughout Perth, with the same kindred spirit to see the lost won to Christ. She also has an advisory board of seven, with two more pastors on that board, to oversee the general running of her ministry. These boards are there to see that everything is done decently and in order. She welcomes the wealth of wisdom and practical advice that comes from the formation of such boards, deliberately making herself accountable to others more mature in ministry than she is.

And to further cloak her ministry in a covering mantle, she was officially ordained to the ministry in early 1991 by Pastor Ray McCauley of Rhema, South Africa, in the presence of her own Pastor, Phillip Baker of Rhema, Perth. Officially she bears the title, 'the Reverend Margaret Court', but like anything that hints of being a little ostentatious, Margaret prefers to leave that title on her ordination certificate. Margaret had been across to Pastor McCauley's church some years before to speak in the highly successful *Night of Champions* sporting night. She had long respected Pastor McCauley, a former 'Mr Universe' finalist in body building, for his uncompromising stand for God: a stand not unlike her own. Today he has a position of prominence in that nation, being one of the few 'religious' leaders invited to be present at the important peace talks between the various dissenting groups. He proclaims a call to unity and a call to repentance, believing that South Africa must seek God as never before, as the answer to its ugly, racial problems. Just as Ray is called to South Africa, Margaret knows she is called to her own nation Australia; again to call for its repentance and a return to God and righteousness.

To avoid any accusation from either the Church or the secular world that she has profited personally from her ministry – especially as it grows in size and influence – she has established it into an incorporated body. This puts her own personal wealth and assets, gained long before she ever thought of going into ministry, outside the financial side of the ministry. Thus the ministry is a non-profit-making one, giving to those who have little to give.

Her ministry team are all committed, mature Christians. Twenty-six men and women, from all different denominations, who give voluntarily of their time and freely of their love. Margaret sees each member as an important part of her ministry 'team', for they each contribute their own particular gift to the ministry.

'I could not do it without them,' she readily admits. God had shown her that she was to 'captain' this team by her own example, always encouraging, guiding, and teaching them the principles of leadership and responsibility. It really was very similar to the days when she as captain, had taken the younger members of the Australian Federation Cup team under her wing. She had considered that appointment as a great honour and felt no less honoured by heading up God's team. Right from the start Margaret felt that she was to use her leadership skills to prepare her own team to eventually go out into their own ministries. This would also ensure that the labourers in God's harvest-fields would continue to increase, as these went out and trained up others the way she had trained them.

Margaret knows that the vision given to her by God, has to be put into the heart of her team if they are to fulfil the major aims of the ministry. The imparting of that vision to each of them, will assure success, for a house united will surely stand. In sport a team can only play well if they are united together, and have a clear understanding of their aims and the most effective way to achieve them.

The ministry team already have an inherent unity from being members of the same 'family'. The foremost aim and the core of the vision is to lead the lost, the lonely and the hurting to a personal and loving relationship with Jesus Christ. There is only one way that aim can be attained, and that is through love; the type of pure, unconditional love that Jesus said would never fail.

Gifts of food, finances, bedding and clothing are distributed to those in need, practically demonstrating the love of God in a tangible way. All finances received, either in the free-will offerings or from donations to the ministry, are always put back into the ministry. The money is used to purchase the various items and to cover the inherent costs of the ministry operations. Surplus funds are sown back into other mission work, both in Perth and overseas.

Well over thirty meetings have now been held at the time this book goes to print. Each meeting is unique, as the Holy Spirit moves through Margaret in different ways to meet the various needs of all those in attendance. This invariably leads the lost, lonely and the hurting, to a personal relationship with Jesus Christ, the fulfilment of the ministry's major aim.

Since the first public meeting in the Perth suburb of Kallaroo in March 1991, over a hundred people have given their lives to Christ for the first time. Many others have re-dedicated their lives back to Christ, after going through what could be best described as a 'wilderness' experience. Another one hundred and fifty have been baptised in the Holy Spirit, with the evidence of speaking in a new tongue.

Defeated, depressed and downtrodden lives are constantly being changed in every meeting. Testimonies abound, and none is more dramatic than that of Martin, who tells of his own powerful conversion to Christianity the night Margaret taught on the love and character of God.

'I was desperate. I really did not know what I could do to salvage my marriage which was in crisis. For a long time I had hungered for the reality of God and had sought Him in many alternate ways and practices but, always, I came up dry and empty. I became hard and had not cried for many years. In many ways I just went about my life, totally absorbed in my own selfish interests, ignoring my wife and family. But it all suddenly went wrong, when I found that my wife was looking for the love and affection that I was not giving to her, elsewhere.

'I rang a Christian friend, who suggested I go and hear Margaret Court speak. Although I was not a Christian, I was an avid squash player and the thought of hearing Margaret Court was a real bonus. If she had no answers for me in what she preached then, at least, I would get to hear from the champion herself. But the minute she spoke, warm, powerful waves came over me, and when an invitation was given for people to come forward and be set free in their lives by receiving Jesus I couldn't get to the front quickly enough. I knew, I don't really know how, that Jesus was the way, the truth and the life; the answer to all those years of seeking. I knew I needed Jesus to come into my life and transform me into a better person. As she prayed for me I could not help but cry. Somehow it felt like my tears were ushering in a new and better life and at the same time washing away the old life. My wife, who had agreed to come with me in a final attempt to salvage our marriage, was amazed at the sight of those tears. In all our twenty years of marriage she had only ever seen me cry on one occasion – the day my dog died! Today our marriage is totally restored, better than it was before and I proudly sit beside my wife and two daughters in the same church as Margaret. I truly believe my conversion to Christianity was nothing short of miraculous. That meeting was my Damascus Road and I will be eternally grateful to Margaret for introducing me to Jesus – the answer to all my problems.'

There was not one dry eye in the hall, in the night meeting, when Jim stood to his feet and told his poignant story of a young life, orphaned from the age of four, shattered by abandonment, rejection and chronic child abuse.

'I trusted no-one and hated everyone – especially God, who had allowed such hurt and heartache in my life, under the hands of those who professed to be his servants,' he candidly related. 'When I was old enough, if fifteen can be termed old enough, I turned to alcohol to numb the pain and anaesthetise me to the pain and hurt of my lonely world. I hardened my heart and determined that nothing would ever again hurt me and became very hostile and aggressive towards everything and everyone. It was not long before I went to prison for my aggressive behaviour. I had married, but of course that did not last, for I did not know how to love anyone. In all my life I had never heard a single soul say the three most precious words "I love you" to me. For fifty years it has been the same story.'

But Jim's story would have a wonderful conclusion as he told of the day he decided to go to a Margaret Court meeting: a day he would later describe as 'the best day in his whole life'. Jim had actually given up drinking at this stage but he was still a very lost and lonely soul.

'Margaret spoke about the love of God being able to heal all the hurts and rejections of the past if a person could forgive everyone who had hurt them,' Jim recalled. 'I was totally overwhelmed by the love and genuine warmth that seemed to flow from Margaret. She spoke as if she really knew God as a loving, heavenly Father, and I wanted that too. At the end of the meeting, she invited all those who had been hurt, wounded and bruised to go forward and receive prayer. I had to go forward because the love pulled me.' He wept, as he recalled the enormous emotion of that day. Going on, he further told of those feelings he had as he went forward. 'When Margaret prayed with me, I felt the love of God go right through my body and pierce my hardened heart. I willingly received Jesus Christ as my Lord and Saviour, right there and then, for I knew He had just healed my broken heart. Immediately, I knew that I would be able to forgive all those who had ever hurt me and be free of the painful memories of the past. Margaret had spoken, that same night, that to be free to love and be loved there had to be no areas of unforgiveness in our lives; regardless of the situation. "Forgiveness will bring your healing" she said, "for as God has forgiven you of much, so you need to forgive others of much. Don't let unforgiveness get into your heart; give it all to God. He knows all about it and He alone is the avenger. Let it all go, for it will surely destroy you.""

Jim then told of how he was able to go from that meeting and in the weeks following, search out all those early educators and tell them he had forgiven them, and ask for their forgiveness for his hatred towards them. He continued to come to the meetings, and after hearing how he could start to use faith in his life to have his every need met, Jim ended his moving testimony that night by introducing his bride of just two months. He said, 'For the first time I know how it feels to be really loved.'

Today Jim is a happy 'newlywed', attending a solid Christian church; his past life truly gone as he walks in the newness of his life in Christ.

Annie, a recent arrival from Britain told of having many financial miracles happen in a short time as she attended a meeting where Margaret taught that every need, even financial, can be met by believing and acting on God's word. One lady told of how her headaches had totally disappeared as she sat and listened to Margaret teach the word on healing. Another lady with severe depression was healed in the same way. One young man who took a morning off work to attend a meeting was healed of a long-standing back ailment. Margaret always emphasises the truth that the glory belongs to God, for she knows that she can do nothing, and is nothing, without Him. Still there is a gratitude that comes from all the people to whom she ministers. For they know it is her great love for them and her willingness and obedience to bring them the gospel, that has been the turning point in their lives; and for some that has meant the difference between life and death.

Others have written letters to the ministry, sharing their good news and declaring their heart-felt gratitude. This letter from Susan is one such letter.

'Dear Margaret and the ministry team,
During the last six months I began to feel unwell with symptoms that would come and go. I consulted my doctor who diagnosed a chemical imbalance in my body; this was due to the brain not regulating certain chemicals in my body properly. This imbalance was caused by a crash diet I went on twelve years previously for which I was hospitalised and given medical treatment. The only treatment my doctor could give me was drugs, which he felt reluctant to do because of my age.

During the month of July I went to a Margaret Court meeting. Margaret prayed for me and Jesus healed me! Since that night I have felt completely different. I now have plenty of energy; I feel whole and well on the inside.

I know Jesus is real and he does heal today.

He heals physically, emotionally, mentally and spiritually. He knows everything there is to know about a person and each of their needs. He wants to make them free and whole. I know this is true because Jesus healed me.

Susan Stone'

Many people can tell similar stories, of having a particular need met through Margaret's ministry. But more than that Margaret knows they must learn as she did, the spiritual principles of 'why' they received as they did, and how it was all made possible through Jesus Christ. Each person who makes a decision for Christ is further encouraged to attend a local church which preaches God's word, and not religious traditions. Here the principles which they have often received but not fully understood, can be taught and expanded in a living, caring fellowship.

Margaret's ministry provides an encouraging nucleus of strong, loving support and teaching, for those who are not ready to stand alone. This discipleship is perhaps the greatest thrust of her ministry. She knows that many who receive no further knowledge will perish – as she almost did – if the word of God is not built into them. The counselling team contact and visit with all those who have urgent needs and who require a little more support.

Nothing is done in her ministry without prayer going forth to prepare the path ahead. The ministry team pray before each meeting to break down the barriers of resistance to the word going forth, and to accomplish the salvation of all those who would be attending. The years she spent heading the intercessory prayer groups have seen her develop into a mighty prayer warrior who knows when, how and what to pray, for her finely tuned spiritual antennae is so sensitive to the Holy Spirit.

The people that come and receive in the meetings, are those for whom she and her team have already prayed – sometimes with tears – and believed God for. God will often reveal those who are in pain or suffering from feelings of despair and hopelessness, long before the actual meetings, so that the snare that is holding them in bondage is broken, and they are free to receive in the meeting. Margaret sees every single person as valuable and precious to God. She sees them with His heart of mercy, compassion and love. She listens caringly and with understanding; never judging, just giving out the wisdom of God from His word that she knows will change any situation from defeat into victory.

She has a heart for families and is truly saddened by the breakdown of the family; whatever the relationship. She sees divorce as a type of cancer eating into the hearts of men, women and children everywhere. Her ministry has as one of its principal goals, a desire to bring back family groups together in the unity of love and fellowship.

The family unit is the one that Margaret desires to see restored and repaired in the love of Christ. A nation is only as strong as its building blocks; societies made up of strong family units. The family unit is under attack in Australia, as it is all over the world, through the breakdown of marriages. Divorce has become the nation's most practised acivity with a failure rate topping fifty percent of first time marriages. Second and third marriages do nothing to reduce the percentage favourably as they fail quicker at a far greater rate. Margaret ministers in this area, believing that pride and unforgiveness; the inability to say 'I'm sorry', is often the principal reason behind most marriage breakdowns.

Margaret, like so many others, faced the possibility of a crisis in her own marriage in the early years because she did not want to 'give in' on any issue if she felt she was justified. Her stubborn streak was well known. She had only been married a short time when she had a disagreement with Barry. Not satisfied with the way the argument developed, or rather didn't develop as Barry would not be drawn in, she withdrew into a shell of sulky silence, refusing to discuss the matter further. She busied herself and pretended not to notice Barry, secretly hoping he'd ask her something and then she would ignore him. But Barry simply walked up to her and said in his abrupt, honest manner, 'Now, we'll have no more of that sort of behaviour around here. If you've got something to say, say it and get it off your chest.'

Nobody had ever brought her face to face with her moodiness as abruptly as Barry. She, like most champion athletes was prone to mood swings almost without knowing it. They came with the stress, nature and outcome of competition; the inherent highs and lows that came from celebrating a win or lamenting a loss. Withdrawal had become a way of life, for she had often withdrawn, to focus totally on a game ahead. Also, she had always avoided publicity, being terribly fearful of public speaking; so she rarely learnt to voice her strongly held opinions, choosing to keep them deep within.

Barry's direct statement took her by surprise, but she quickly saw that he had hit on the real crux of the matter. She had not liked the tension between them any better than he had, and immediately saw how childish her behaviour was in the light of his words. She apologised and resolved not to let anything that was in her heart against Barry stay there and build into resentment. She loved Barry and she knew he loved her, and she saw that it was foolish to have hostile, unspoken words of resentment between them. She shares that her marriage is good because for the next twenty five years of their married life she felt free to be open and honest with Barry, and so they rarely had bad words between them. Forgiveness freely flowed; she was always ready to say 'I'm sorry, please forgive me,' as was Barry, who did not know how to hold a grudge.

Margaret and Barry always had a firm belief in the sanctity and the commitment of their marriage vows, long before they became Christians. Christianity simply strengthened and confirmed their belief that marriage is ordained of God. Margaret sees the relationship she has with Barry as a physical bond; the relationship she has with God is a spiritual bond.

A good marriage will combine the physical and the spiritual into a godly unit that no man can put asunder. Likewise a strong, Christian life will combine the spiritual with the physical to ensure success in all areas of life.

Margaret feels strongly that such important commitments as marriage and accepting Christ, should be done publicly before a crowd of witnesses. Marriage is an oath taken before witnesses and accepting Jesus should also be before witnesses. She feels that private commitments, like New Year's resolutions, soon lose their convictions. She has no time for those who are afraid to confess Jesus publicly with the excuse that religion is a very private matter.

To have a truly successful marriage, each partner has to 'die' to self and esteem the other more highly than themself. Likewise to have a truly successful Christian life, a person needs to die to self also. Death to self means that Christ could surely live within and the union would surely live; this time eternally.

Margaret often shares these godly principles for marriage, for inherent in them are the basics of the unity that must come into the current, segmented and divided Body of Christ, if the world is going to be won to Christ. In a far greater sense, death must come to all would-be servants of Christ, for the Body of Christ to rise and live and be greater than any single denomination or individual.

That Margaret operates under a powerful anointing of the Holy Spirit comes as no surprise to those who have received from that anointing. Many fall under the anointing in her meetings, through the powerful presence of God, the word, and the Holy Spirit residing within her.

That anointing, which is the powerful, overwhelming sensation of the presence of God, is not always apparent, either to her or those she ministers to, for the Holy Spirit is free to move as He wills through her.

The gifts of the Spirit are manifested in her meetings, because she has asked for them to flow, and is obedient to let them flow. The gifts are there to meet the needs of the people: to allow them to receive from God what they need. That anointing is always there, as she teaches the word, lays hands on the sick, prophesies, speaks forth with an utterance in tongues to be interpreted, or simply holds someone in a loving embrace. God moves with different manifestations of His power through her sensitivity and obedience to do as He wills. He knows only too well that everyone is different and will receive in a different manner.

Not only does Margaret operate in the gifts of the Spirit but so too does her team. She constantly tells them to desire the gifts to meet the needs of the people for which they are designed.

This ministry is not unique; there are many others throughout the world that are bringing forth the same truths that she does, and who do it in like manner with an outreaching, evangelistic thrust to the poor. But a steady stream of love from the ministry team in all their areas, has characterised this ministry as a ministry of love. This love has been said to have been 'tangible', as people have walked through the doors. Many a reason given, in later testimonies, as to why a life was surrendered to Christ has often been ... 'because for the first time in my life I felt really loved, wanted and accepted, just as I was...'

This is the greatest compliment that Margaret and the whole ministry team can be given. This is the love that motivated her original establishment of the ministry, and this is the love that she desires to see continue in the work of the ministry. This is the unconditional, self-sacrificing love that Jesus said would show people His true disciples; those doing the work of reconciling a defeated world to Him, by showing the love of God that never fails.

Chapter Eight

Finale

In July 1992, Margaret celebrated her 50th birthday and a testimonial night was given in her honour, to which people who had in some way impacted her life were invited. Speeches were given from three different groups of people – her tennis partners and coaches, ministry and church associates including her ministry team, and family members. Many only knew one particular side to her life but there were those, like Barry, Anne and Helen, who were involved in all three of the major aspects.

All made mention of her never-say-die attitude and determination, her trustworthiness, and her loyalty and value as a true and trusted friend. The sporting fraternity in particular, made issue of the fact that Margaret always displayed a stubborn determination to perfect any task she undertook. Former practise players and coaches made mention of the fact that she worked harder and longer than any other individual they had ever known, to get to the top in tennis. But the comments made by those who know her best – her own children – best describe the type of person she really is.

Lisa, her youngest daughter, told the large crowd in attendance that her mother had always been there for her whenever she had needed her. Her mum had never let her down.

And not only was she always there for Lisa, and the other family members, but she was also there for anybody who needed her to be a friend, helper or counsellor. Her recently completed beautiful new home, built on the same site as the former house, adjacent to the magnificent Swan River, is the proverbial oasis to those who find themselves buffeted by the inevitable storms of life. Indeed, the sheer numbers of people that sought her help in the sanctuary of her home, prompted her move into ministry, for she did not want her home to be too disrupted by the continual influx of visitors.

The people who came with their problems never left her home disappointed, for she always seemed to be able to give a word in season; the word they needed desperately to hear at that stage. She always had a seemingly bottomless reservoir of God's word within her.

'The word always works,' she would encourage the person, knowing that the word she gave would often cut through to the root of the problem far more than any long sympathetic discussions or detailed analysis of the problem. 'Always speak the desired answer, not the problem,' she counselled.

Her second youngest child Teresa, made mention of the fact that her mother did all the chores that no-one really sees or truly appreciates. And indeed, Margaret Court is an ordinary wife and mother, with the same family related chores and activities as anybody else.

She often relates in her meetings that she has cooked the family breakfast, made the beds, put out the washing and driven her children to school, just hours before she ministers. During the school holiday periods she can be found at the family property doing a large amount of cooking for the shearing teams. She wants people to see that she is not a spiritual 'guru', too spiritual to be any earthly good. She knows all about the pressure of raising a family and living in today's world. She is not, and believes all ministers should not be, removed from the realities of life. But into all of the mundane chores and endless family tasks, she brings Christ.

'I don't separate my life into the sacred and the secular. Every day and every task can be totally rewarding if it is always done with the right heart motive of love. I can talk to God as freely when I am doing the ironing as much as when I go to be alone with him in my study. God does not want me to be someone different than what I am all the time.'

Marika, her eldest daughter and the potential athlete of the family, noticed that although they were a family of six, more often than not they had ten or more for dinner! This is the generous side of her mother who would always share everything, and make everyone feel welcome in their home.

Margaret has no qualms about enjoying an obviously comfortable existence. 'Having material possessions isn't the problem,' she says. 'It's the love of things that is the real problem. The more you have, the more you can give away.' And indeed, she lives by this sound biblical principle, believing that God prospers His people so they in turn can help others less fortunate. Barry has that same generous nature, willing to share, help or assist anyone, anytime.

Great howls of laughter echoed around the hall as twenty-year old Daniel, Margaret's only son and eldest child remarked that his mum was the best mum he could possibly have! A big grin appeared when he realised that she was the *only* mum he would ever have. Unashamedly he told his mum that he loved her. Coming from a fully grown young man, that was a great witness to all who were in attendance that night. Margaret knows that her ministry begins in her home and works its way outward to the public. She does not act any differently when she is away from home, as when she is at home. She does not wear a ministry mask of 'holiness' to hide any areas of impropriety in her own personal life. She is careful to treat her own family well and not subject them to any outbursts of anger, selfishness or the neglect that familiarity often breeds. She is acutely aware there is no alternative to constantly walking in love and forgiveness at all times. And she has taught her family to ask for forgiveness always if strife and arguments have broken out.

'It doesn't matter who is right or who is wrong. Be quick to say you're sorry for your part,' she teaches them, for she knows that this 'clearing the air' of unforgiveness is vital in creating a loving, strong family. Unforgiveness is the principal cause of most broken family relationships. True love is really being able to forgive, time and time again; something that every family has opportunity to test every day.

Her sole motivation is to serve God by showing her love to a world that is in desperate need of the answers that can be found in accepting Christ as the Lord and Saviour of their lives.

Margaret Court is not a manufactured personality. She is as you find her; a friendly, statuesque woman with a great love for people, reflecting her great love of God. She considers herself an ordinary wife and mother, although she may be justified in esteeming herself more highly in light of her tremendous tennis achievements. She portrays no sign of an inflated ego, just a healthy self-esteem of who and what she is in Christ.

She always saw her tennis ability as a gift from God; one that many other people were also given but did not develop as she had. She coupled that gifted natural talent with a fierce determination to put her name into the world's record books, which, of course she did. It's amazing to consider that no other tennis player, woman or man, has ever equalled her record of twenty-four single Grand Slam titles, and probably never will. It's a most impressive way to be immortalised in tennis history.

She herself never exalts the achievement of any person who is naturally gifted. It is the endeavour they exhibit in developing their talent that meets with her approval. She always found it hard to be treated as someone special just because she could play tennis well. It was something she was good at and wanted to do. It didn't make her a better person, nor did it qualify her to speak as an authority on issues of some magnitude, as sports stars today are often asked to do.

Tennis influenced her exterior world; but it never changed her on the inside as a person, where she felt there was something missing. It didn't matter that she was successful, famous and reasonably wealthy. That something was always missing, until she met Jesus Christ. Jesus made all the difference. She knows that it is only Jesus, and He alone, that can change the nature of the heart.

This is the message that she is taking to the City of Perth and ultimately to her nation, Australia. This is the message that will change and transform lives as it did hers. This is the message that will bring temporal victory and eternal salvation. This is the message that God has committed to her, and others like her, to take to the nations.

That she is a woman in ministry; once thought to be totally male-orientated, is not even a factor in her thinking. God calls, God equips and God provides the gift that is obviously in her, for ministry. Jesus said that those who were truly His, would be known from the fruit of their labour in life and ministry.

This fruit, evidenced in Margaret's ministry, is testimony in itself that she is truly called of God.

A life of example and a ministry of love and excellence, are the priorities that dominate her life. She desires to do everything she does to the best of her ability; to develop her God-given talents to their fullest. She desires to cultivate the true shepherd's heart for the sheep of the flock and to search out all those who are without the True Shepherd.

She is not into competition; those days are long behind her. She sees her ministry as a part of the Body of Christ, doing its part, so that the whole Body can function as a whole. This is the type of unity that she prays will come in the world wide Body of Christ for it is the unity that Christ said would characterise his Church in the last days. Denominational walls are barriers to true unity and must come down for an unhindered flow of the Holy Spirit. As they come down, so will the echelons of established, lifeless religions and each person can do their part in reconciling the world to Jesus. It is not a commission given to the 'clergy', but to the true disciples of Christ; men and women everywhere, who desire to serve Him in the liberty of the Holy Spirit. Margaret Court is one such disciple.

The Prayer

For thirty years I sat in a church pew. No-one ever told me that I needed to make a decision to ask Jesus Christ into my life as my own personal Saviour and Lord.

The Bible clearly states in Romans 10:9 and 10, that if you confess the Lord Jesus with your mouth and believe in your heart that God has raised Jesus from the dead, you will be *saved*. For with the mouth confession is made unto salvation and with the heart belief is made unto righteousness.

By praying the following prayer, out loud, and believing it in your heart, you will have the same assurance that I have today, of eternal life.

'Heavenly Father, I believe *Jesus* is your *Son* and that you raised Him from the dead. I thank you that you have forgiven and forgotten all my past mistakes; that old things have passed away and all things are now new. I am now born again. I have new life right from this moment. I have eternal life now in the name of Jesus and I thank you for it. Amen.'   (2 Corinthians 5:17)

Congratulations and welcome to the family of God. I urge you to join a Word-based church to grow in the things of God. Please write and tell us of this wonderful decision you have made today.

Margaret Court Ministries
37 Florence Road
Nedlands 6009
Western Australia

I pray God's peace and protection on you and your family, and pray for success in everything you purpose to do in life.

Margaret Court